DEDICATION

For Brooke and Ethan my Love, Light, and Joy. May we find each other again and again. And for Michael, thank you for all that you gave.

STEP
INTO THE
GAP

Where Peace Of Mind Allows
You To Take On Life

TESSA ARNOLD

As someone who has written about and teaches the concept of *"standing in the gap,"* I know firsthand how vital this conversation is—especially in today's world where women are rising into leadership and power in unprecedented ways. Tessa Arnold's Step Into the Gap is not just timely; it's transformational.

With the wisdom of a seasoned executive and the soul of a healer, Tessa bridges the divide between achievement and authenticity. Her journey from high-powered finance to holistic wellness is inspiring, and her method—rooted in mindfulness, intuition, and identity—offers a roadmap for women navigating the complex spaces between roles, expectations, and self.

This book is a powerful guide for any woman who is seeking alignment, peace, and purpose while striving for success. Tessa gives us permission to pause, to reflect, and most importantly, to step into the space where our true power lives.

Tessa, thank you for this work. The world needs it.

— *Lisa Chastain, Top Money Coach for Women | Author of Stop Budgeting, Start Living | Host of Real Money Podcast*

Tessa's groundbreaking book highlights perfectly the practices we MUST embrace to step into our potential. Her genuine and genius approach helps us all actualize – becoming the best versions of ourselves. When we're our best, everyone thrives.

— *Angie Morgan, Marine Veteran, NY Times Best-Selling Author, and Take the Lead creator*

Tessa Arnold's *Step Into the Gap* is a powerful guide for anyone seeking greater clarity, resilience, and alignment in their lives. Drawing from her own transformation from finance executive to wellness expert, Tessa offers a unique system that blends ancient wisdom with modern mindfulness techniques. Her insights into the space between thoughts, the interplay of ego and intuition, and the pressures that pull us away from our true selves are both enlightening and practical. Step Into the Gap is an essential read for those ready to unlock their fullest potential and create a more meaningful, balanced life.

— Dr. Kate Lund, Clinical Psychologist

CONTENTS

Dedication .... *iii*

Chapter One: What is the Gap? 1

Chapter Two: The Importance of Identity 17

Chapter Three: The Struggle for Women Today 39

Chapter Four: Awareness of the Gap 57

Chapter Five: The Process of Stepping into the Gap 75

Chapter Six: Expanding the Moment 97

Chapter Seven: Your Self within the Gap 113

Chapter Eight: Making the Gap a Habit 129

Chapter Nine: Proactively Supporting your Future Self 145

Chapter Ten: Core Relationships through the Gap 161

Chapter Eleven: The Path to Leadership and
Power through the Gap 177

About Author *191*

Chapter One

WHAT IS THE GAP?

The bathroom is a sanctuary. I know I cannot be alone in thinking this. It is a place where a mother can snatch just five minutes of time away from the seemingly constant needs of others.

It's a refuge for a teenage girl with overbearing brothers, where she can play music and sing in the shower. It's a healing spa where a laborer can soak his exhausted limbs in a hot bath.

It is where I used to go to cry, when I was a little girl. When the stream of confusion and fear that ran through my young life swelled and broke its banks, I would seek out the safety of the bathroom and let go of my tears.

I would do the kind of sobbing you only ever do alone. (Even in the safest company, the presence of another human often makes us stop short of letting go completely. It is scary to make yourself that vulnerable.) Then, after the tears subsided, I would sit peacefully and embrace that wonderful feeling that comes after a good cry. Some people call it "post-cry clarity," where the problems that sent you spiraling now seem less daunting. You have achieved a healing sense of perspective.

What is so special about the bathroom in these scenarios? And let's be clear, it doesn't actually need to be a bathroom. I know of friends who retreated under the bed to cry as children, or clambered into a closet.

Perhaps it's the solitude and security of space. You are alone; no one is there to hurt you or judge you. You are in a cave, shielded from the elements; you are cocooned within a warm, nurturing womb.

You have punctuated your day with a respite from the madness of the world. Your time in the bathroom is the space between two painful words. It is the gap between one demand and the next.

Though let's be honest. There's only so many times you can visit the bathroom in a day. You cannot live your life constantly seeking refuge in physical spaces. But what if there were a way to find that peace whenever you wanted? What if there were a way to step into that gap, between manic moments (chaos incarnate) and placid ones (where the world is still)?

It turns out there *is* a way to do this. There is a method by which you can access those moments of calm, at any time you please. And I discovered this superpower when my life was falling apart.

From the outside, I would have appeared fine. More than fine. I had been married for ten years with two beautiful children. I was in my mid-thirties and had already built up a successful career working for a global bank, with a portfolio of clients that I traveled regularly to meet.

However, the reality was different. Like many career-driven women, I appeared to the outside world as thriving, when in reality, I was barely surviving. My relationship with my husband was on life support, and the demands of parenting two young toddlers while balancing an incredibly stressful job sometimes felt too much to bear.

I felt like a failure in my relationship when we began the divorce process, and I was terrified that my next failure would be as a parent, in meeting the needs of my children. Those things that define a stereotypically fulfilling life —a marriage, children, a high-flying career—sometimes felt as much a burden as a privilege. The weight of these responsibilities became hard to bear, and I did not have the time necessary to train my body and mind to withstand this accumulation.

I was hemorrhaging energy, and there was no opportunity to replenish my resources. I became a shell of a human. I would look in the mirror and not even recognize myself. Who was this tense, scowling creature looking back at me?

The tension in my mind began to spread like a colonizing force, taking over my neck, back, and shoulders. I could no longer stand up straight and suffered chronic pain.

I was in complete survival mode, on autopilot, just trying to get from one moment to the next, trying to keep myself together, and stop myself from imploding under the pressure of...life. How is this who I had become? Why was I unable to enjoy and manage the life I had worked so hard to achieve? Why had so many of life's gifts seemingly transformed into curses?

I couldn't put on a brave face any longer. I wanted to scream; I wanted to beat my hands against the wall. Within this maelstrom I found myself retreating to an old refuge. As I did in childhood, I went into the bathroom, closed the door, and let the banks break.

I sought out the solitude and comfort of that little space, where I allowed myself to fall to pieces before putting myself back together again. I was surprised at the level of comfort it gave me. But it was, of course, impractical. I could hardly schedule intermittent bathroom or closet-bound crying sessions in my daily routine.

And then it dawned on me. What if instead of seeking out a physical space for a sort of emotional reset, I found a metaphorical space in which to seek refuge? What might that even look like?

I thought about why moving from one physical space to another—such as from my living room into my bathroom—had such a profound impact on me.

The effect that switching physical spaces has on our brains can be observed through phenomena such as the Doorway Effect. We've all been there—you need to grab something from the living room, but as soon as you walk through the doorway, you forget what you were searching for.

This is because the brain holds on to moment-to-moment memories for a short period of time, purging these memories when new stuff comes along. Walking into a new space can trigger this memory purge. Additionally, when you say, "I need to get my car keys from the living room," in reality, that singular thought is the beginning of an increasingly important set of concerns. What you are really saying to yourself is, "I need to get my car keys from the living room so I can drive to the office and work in order to receive a paycheck so I can maintain a household and provide for my children who have developing needs."

When you pass through the doorway, switching rooms, the context of your train of thought might get jolted and jump further along the hierarchy of concerns. You are no longer thinking about your keys; you're thinking about what you are going to make the kids for dinner that night. Researchers have found that the Doorway Effect is a phenomena that occurs with metaphorical boundaries as well (i.e., memory can be disrupted by imagining the act of walking through a doorway).

The act of transitioning from one space into another had a strong psychological impact on me. By entering the bathroom in my state of childhood distress, I was closing a door on the outside world and giving myself time to breathe in that brief period—that gap—before I had to face my next challenge.

Where could I find the metaphorical transition from room to room within my own mind? What could I think about that would bring on this effect? Perhaps it wasn't a thought at all. Perhaps, I began to suspect, it was at the threshold between thoughts themselves.

This was the most powerful personal insight I have ever had, and it has had a transformational effect on my life. Increasingly, I began to focus on the gap between thoughts, and I learned how to step right into this gap, occupying its space. These gaps were some of the most serene and calm places my mind had ever experienced. I realized that if I perfected this mental exercise, it could have a profound impact on the way I function.

To give you an idea of what I mean, let me provide an analogy. Imagine two people, a boy and a girl, swimming in the ocean. At first, the ocean is calm; but soon, waves begin to pick up. They crash down upon the shore with increasing frequency and intensity. The boy is an inexperienced swimmer and begins to panic. When a wave approaches, he attempts to outswim it, retreating back toward the shore with manic, inefficient strokes of his arms and legs. His attempt is futile, of course, and the wave engulfs him; he tumbles about as if inside a washing machine, struggling to locate up from down. As soon as the wave subsides and he is able to draw a few breaths, another wave pounds on top of his head, forcing him back into the water.

The girl, meanwhile, is a strong swimmer and knows how the ocean behaves. When a wave approaches, she swims toward it, ducking down into the water as it passes over her, and popping up behind the wave like a seal. She now has the luxury of a dozen or so seconds before the next wave arrives. She can fill her lungs with large breaths and gather herself. She may even look out to enjoy the view across the horizon, as the sunlight shimmers across the open water.

The ocean cannot be tamed, of course, and the tide will never cease. But because she is able to rest in the gaps between waves, she can take each one as it comes without becoming overwhelmed or pulled under like the helpless boy.

For me, the inevitable tide of my thoughts had become unmanageable, and I was drowning. I was letting the more aggressive thoughts bash me around, drag me under, and before I could respond or address one thought, another was on top of me. And like with the ocean, there was no let up. The average person has around 6,000 thoughts per day, according to a study from Queen's University in Canada published in Nature Communications. There was only one thing for it. I needed to become a better swimmer. I needed to utilize the space between waves, or thoughts, to my advantage.

Focusing on the space between thoughts, or "stepping into the gap" as I call it, has allowed me to approach my life and my problems with radical agency. It has helped me organize my priorities and address my problems in a manageable way.

I realized that, in some way, I had been stepping into the gap my whole life. Retreating into the bathroom as a child was a prime example. But now I was able to do it on a mental level, and the support it provided was unparalleled.

This might seem like relatively unconventional thinking for someone who had spent over a decade working in the financial services industry. But the truth is, I have always been fascinated by understanding health and wellbeing on a deep and holistic level.

As well as being an experienced VP for divisions of two major American banks, I am also a fully trained Ayurvedic health coach. Ayurveda is essentially a 5,000-year-old body of knowledge that encourages us to center our lives around six pillars to achieve harmony of body and mind. These are: food or nutrition; sleep; nourishing and cleansing; movement; breathing and stress management; and self-awareness and self-reflection.

Around the time of the global COVID-19 pandemic, I found myself thinking ever more deeply about these aspects of life, as was the case for many people. During lockdown, we had more time to look within ourselves, more time for meal preparation, exercise, and thinking about wellbeing. I know people who took up drawing, baking, and practicing mindfulness during this time. It was a devastating period—millions lost their lives and livelihoods. Entire parts of society broke down or were irrevocably changed. But in times of crisis, human beings also innovate and find new opportunities. Many would attest that pandemic lockdowns shone a spotlight on long-neglected aspects of our mental and physical wellbeing.

For some people, this focus on mental and physical harmony took a back seat when the pandemic receded and society reopened incrementally. The opposite was true for me. As the world opened up again, my resolve to actively find wellbeing solutions was stronger than ever.

Finding the space between thoughts prompted a level of self-analysis that bolstered my mental wellbeing. In the ephemeral spaces between ideas, I began asking questions. What do I need to do right now? What is the next right action? What is it that I know in my heart to be true? What is it that's truly going on right now? Why do I feel this way? What even is this emotion? Where's the strength that I need to call upon right now? Is it strength? Or is it a connection that I need?

Within the gap, I find clarity and wisdom. It is a calm and peaceful place, where I feel safe to ask anything. It has allowed me the opportunity to step into myself and ask one of the most important questions of all: "Does something need to change?"

The world is awash with distractions, diversion, and dopamine hits. It is so hard to check in with ourselves and perform any kind of self-analysis when our senses are constantly stimulated. From staring at spreadsheets at work, to doomscrolling TikTok on the couch and streaming Netflix in bed, screens block our ability to look within.

And this behavior is understandable. The stream of 6,000 thoughts a day can become overwhelming. If you don't know how to swim, why even get in the water? If being left with your own thoughts is so daunting, why not plug into a podcast, or thumb through Instagram for hours on end. It might sound counterintuitive, but laying on the sofa and scrolling through social media is not a form of relaxation. You are not "switching off"; instead, you are constantly being bombarded by stressful stimuli. Many studies have linked heavy social media use with increased levels of anxiety and depression.

Conversely, the serene, peaceful pools that exist between our thoughts can be used to our benefit. I would offer that stepping into the gap is an efficient way to elicit the "relaxation response" in people. The relaxation response is the opposite of the "stress response," which is commonly referred to as "fight or flight."

Fight or flight is a powerful physiological response to a threat. It is easy to understand how animals evolved this mechanism: When faced with a perilous situation like an approaching predator, the body primes itself to either attack or flee with great efficacy and urgency. A cascade of stress hormones courses through the body, activating the sympathetic nervous system. The stress response leads to a whole host of physiological changes, including but not limited to increased blood flow, muscle strength, mental activity and even increased rates of blood coagulation.

This response is incredibly useful if, say, you need to leap up a tree to avoid a charging buffalo. But it is perhaps unhelpful when the stress response is triggered by bad drivers, rising utility bills, misbehaving children, or relationship issues.

The relaxation response, meanwhile, describes the body returning to normal after fight or flight. The parasympathetic nervous system takes over once more; blood pressure, hormone levels, and digestive function all return to normal. The relaxation response will occur naturally after a period of high stress, and there are measures we can take which bring about the response more swiftly. These include things like breathing techniques, meditation, yoga, and tai chi.

I believe that stepping into the gap is another such way to bring about the relaxation response. Dipping into the still waters between thoughts returns us to a state of balance and homeostasis. What's more, we can step into the gap whenever we want. It is available to all of us, instantly.

And stepping into the gap provides us with closure, which is a helpful tool when it comes to moving on from stressful situations. Like closing the bathroom door creates a distinct sanctuary, acknowledging the gaps between thoughts allows us to notice where one thought ends and another begins. This makes things more bearable. Instead of issues clumping together and arriving en masse like a volley of arrows, each problem that comes our way is a discrete and manageable entity.

In this book, I hope to not only convince you that the gap exists but also guide you in stepping into it. I want to show you how to use this method to calm yourself, and how to harness your full potential. In the space between thoughts, you will find questions, answers, and actions that provide you with the support you need to help your present and future self.

You will be able to draw on your knowledge and wisdom, as well as better follow your intuition. You will be able to craft a more hopeful vision of the future, a more truthful understanding of the present, and a more constructive relationship with the past.

These are all the incredible things that can be found in the gap, and they are all available to you right now. I am just here to guide you and teach you how to utilize this superpower.

Once you have grown proficient at using these methods, I will then encourage you to map out a vision of how you want your life to be, including ways in which you are going to show up for yourself and others. You are going to decide what you are going to offer and put out into the world. And then you're going to harness the power of what it is to truly be you. You are going to completely accept and honor yourself as you step out into the world.

We will practice together. You will step into the gap time and time again. You will become comfortable there; it will become second nature to you. And then you will perhaps forget about the gap for a while. Things will be good, and you will plod along with no apparent need for introspection or the ramping down of your stress response.

And then life will hit you, as it always does, with a curveball. You will feel that familiar rush of stress hormones raising your blood pressure. You will feel the lump in your throat as you look around for a quiet place to fall apart. And then you will remember the gap is there for you. You'll thank yourself for being aware of it and for understanding it and for reading this book.

Once I learned about the gap, it changed my whole life, and it continues to change my life to this day. It helps me through my toughest moments, and it's changed how I see the world. It is a beautiful gift that I have shared with my children and loved ones, and I am so happy that I get the chance to share it with you. It will open limitless doors for you, and you will treasure the support it provides. It will be yours for the rest of your life. So come with me on this journey, and let's step into the gap.

Chapter Two

THE IMPORTANCE
OF IDENTITY

"Mirror, mirror, on the wall…I do not know this woman, not at all."

I stared at my reflection, searching for myself and coming up short.

We take for granted that we can recognize ourselves in the mirror, when it may be a rare trait in the animal kingdom. Less than a dozen species have passed the so-called "mirror self-recognition test." Researchers believe that the test is an indicator of self-awareness, and that it is correlated with higher levels of empathy and altruistic behavior.

The father of the theory of evolution Charles Darwin wondered if apes might recognize themselves after seeing an orangutan consider its reflection in a mirror at a zoo, and the American psychologist Gordon Gallup first took this question to the lab in the 1970s.

Gallup introduced a mirror into a room with a chimpanzee and documented any changes in its behavior. At first, the chimp became agitated and stressed, perhaps confusing its reflection with that of a stranger that might pose a threat. As time passed, the fear of aggression and hostility subsided, and the chimp started to relax. The chimp inspected the mirror, then began to groom itself, apparently using its reflection as a guide. Gallup noted that the chimp practiced self-grooming far more frequently with the mirror in the room than without.

In his 2002 book *The Cognitive Animal,* Gallup wrote that the behavior of his research animals "gave the impression that the chimpanzees had learned to recognize themselves."

These findings were noteworthy, but he needed to improve the test; he needed to make it more focused and leave less room for doubt that the chimps had, in fact, identified themselves.

He anesthetized one of his research animals and dyed a small patch of skin on its forehead. He made sure that the dye was odorless and non-tactile, so when the chimp woke up, it was totally unaware of the marking.

Gallup then placed the mirror back in the room with the chimp, who immediately reached for the marking on its face once it had seen its reflection.

"The effect was dramatic," Gallup said. "The chimpanzees looked at their reflection and guided their fingers to the marks on their faces that could only be seen in the mirror. In addition to touching the marks repeatedly and looking at their fingers, some even smelled their fingers."

Gallup noted that rhesus monkeys failed to reach for the blotch of dye when he ran the same test. After subsequent studies showed certain species—including elephants, orangutans, and dolphins—passed the test, researchers posited that self-recognition was an ability reserved for animals with a large neocortex, a region of the brain associated with higher-order functions like sensory perception, cognition, and spatial reasoning. But some apparently smart species—like gorillas—failed the test; meanwhile, a host of creatures with a wide range of cognitive abilities and limitations appeared to have the power of self-recognition. Some varieties of crabs, fish, and birds have appeared able to recognize themselves in mirrors.

Some researchers suggested that the test itself might be a limiting factor, in that not all animals rely on sight to make sense of the world.

Humans are highly visual animals. If our senses were a band, sight would very much be the lead vocalist, accompanied by back-up singers of smell, taste, touch, sound, and proprioception (our sense of where our body is in space). Meanwhile dogs, who fail the mirror test, rely mostly on hearing and smell to navigate their environment. Researchers have designed special olfactory versions of the self-recognition test, and dogs appear to respond far better in these modified conditions.

What does this tell us about identity? Why is it that pigeons and manta rays and orangutans recognize their reflections, but donkeys and cows do not? Why is it that dogs seem to know their own odor belongs to them, but their own faces trigger no sense of self? Would most animals display a sense of self-awareness if we were able to create the right test, which excited particular senses in just the right way?

Is there a rudimentary understanding of "I" in a manta ray? Is there an inherent sense of "me-ness" in a magpie? If there is an innate sense of identity within each of us, then can we learn to access it and nurture it, and conversely can we neglect it and risk it withering away?

I stared at my reflection in the mirror, searching for answers to these questions and more. There were many versions of me staring back. I saw a wife, whose relationship was crumbling around her. I saw a mother—or the contradiction of a mother—capable of running through walls to protect her children, yet simultaneously too exhausted to make her own bed in the morning. I saw a loving sister and a needy daughter. I saw the many roles I had played in my life, like an actress watching her own show reel. I began to remove that day's makeup, thinking of the stains on the chimps' faces.

Which one of these women's faces was I wiping clean? I couldn't find the "I" looking back at me; the "me-ness" was missing.

A worrying symptom of my identity crisis was a lack of clarity behind my motivations. It was as if I were on autopilot, a high-functioning sleepwalker. I would perform a task or action perfectly well, but if you asked me why I was doing what I was doing, I'd struggle to narrow down my intentions.

I would answer, "This is what I am meant to do," instead of, "This is what I want to do."

There are multitudes of ways to live a life, and yet somehow many of us find ourselves conforming to what is expected of us. We buy the same cars, we purchase similar clothing, we go to the same bars and restaurants, we send our kids to the same schools as the folks within our communities, both geographical and socioeconomic. Maybe this is caused by choice paralysis, or the pressure of social conventions, or a combination of these and other factors. Whatever the case, it can feel easier to take the path of least resistance and mimic the lives of others than it is to express our own identities.

A breakthrough came when I began to ask myself a simple question: Do I feel comfortable? Do I feel comfortable in these clothes, in this car, with these people at this bar?

The gap is a wonderful place to ask yourself these questions. That magical space between thoughts, unpolluted by the opinions of others or the pressures of the outside world. First, pose the question. It's best to start with something small, "Do I feel comfortable in these clothes?" rather than something seismic, "Do I feel comfortable with my partner?"

If the answer is yes, then you can move forward in the knowledge that this aspect of your life is not the source of the tension you are searching for. If the answer is no, then you need to analyze that unease.

Take time to ask this question about as many aspects of yourself as you wish, from the food you are eating to the bars that you go to on the weekends to the friends that you spend your time with. Soon, you will have a mental inventory of your existence, categorized into two columns: those things that sit well with you and cause little friction in your mind, and those things that cause you discomfort and require further attention.

How you act in the case of the latter must be decided on an individual basis. In some cases, it can be an easy fix: a minor wardrobe or dietary adjustment that makes you feel more like yourself. Or it can be more complex, like in the instance of a friendship where a frank and honest appraisal is well overdue.

Whatever the case, this exercise will set you on a path toward true self-discovery. If a habit or a relationship is causing you discomfort, chances are that you entered into it for unsatisfactory or empty reasons. The motivation behind your actions may have been closer to "This is what people do" rather than "This is what I want or need."

As you continue with this mental exercise, you are providing yourself with the training and the foundations needed to ask the Big Question: "Am I comfortable with myself?"

Before I even worked up the courage to step into the gap and ask myself this very question, I had an inkling that the answer would be a resounding "No." The clues were there, like traffic cones dotted along the highway ahead of a recent road accident.

I was incapable of keeping still on the couch or laying by myself in bed awake for any period of time. Sitting with my own thoughts was not a peaceful experience— it filled me with anxiety, and I would use any number of distractions to avoid this situation. Listening to music, busying myself with endless mundane house chores, keeping the television on in the background, anything to drown out the terrifying soundtrack of my own mind.

Eventually, my unhappiness became too much to bear. My thoughts began to scale and peer above the wall of distractions I had so diligently built. They could no longer be ignored. I closed my bedroom door, lay on the bed, stepped into the gap and asked the Big Question.

And the answer came back immediately. A resounding "No." I was not comfortable within my own body. I didn't feel like me. I didn't feel at home in my own skin.

I didn't recognize myself. I felt like I was living life on someone else's terms. I didn't feel authentic. This was the continuing source of discomfort. I was trying to place the real me into a life that did not fit. It was too tight in some places, and I would rub up against it; it was too loose in others, offering no support.

I had to get to the root of this, to unravel this mess and rediscover myself. I had to pass the mirror test and get back to being comfortable once more.

I once watched a client come to a similar realization. It can be a scary thing to realize that you have lost your own identity. But it can also be a huge relief to discover the source of your unease and discomfort.

I had my client, let's call her Phoebe, sit with me at my table—an open, honest space—and we talked.

You could tell she was physically and psychologically uneasy. She fidgeted in the chair, tapped her fingers, and even checked her phone a few times during our discussion.

"Do you find it difficult to relax and sit still?" I asked her, all too familiar with this feeling.

"Maybe, but there is just so much to do," she said.

"When was the last time you sat by yourself in silence?" I asked.

"Like I said, there is always so much to do," she said. "I'm a very active, busy person."

"I believe there is a difference between performing essential tasks and indulging distractions," I pushed on. "For example, we need to go to work and make meals for ourselves. But what do you do when you are relaxing and unwinding?"

She began to describe a routine I knew all too well. The true "Phoebe," the real source of her identity, was calling out from within her, begging to be heard, and daily life was an exercise in drowning out the sound of her cries.

Doomscrolling social media, surfing streamers and cable channels, endlessly organizing and reorganizing cupboards and closets that were just fine the way they had been—these were all, at their root, distractions.

"Something needs to be stimulating or grabbing your attention away from the fact that you just don't want to sit with yourself right now because you don't necessarily want to face what's going on," I eventually offered.

Phoebe cast her eyes downward, as if meeting my gaze would be an unwelcome recognition that I was right.

"And you know what, that's okay," I continued. "This is scary. The most courageous thing you could ever do is work on yourself. And trust me, it was scary for me, too, and it still is when I have to face some of these things. But we can do this. I've done it, and we're going to do it together. The fact that you are here shows me that you have the courage."

She took a deep breath and looked back up at me.

"Okay," she said. "I'm ready."

This consent is necessary. Leading someone on this journey is hard enough when they are willing. Dragging someone along against their will is impossible.

She already knew that something needed to change, otherwise she wouldn't have sought me out. She didn't know what, and she didn't know the direction we were going to go in, but something had to give. And she needed to say the words out loud, as much as I needed to hear them.

"Who are you?" I asked. She looked at me curiously.

"You know who I am," she said. "I'm Phoebe."

"That's just your name," I replied. "And you didn't even give that name to yourself; someone else first used that word to describe you. You have the chance now to describe yourself in your own words. So use some of your own words right now. Who are you?"

She sat there for a minute and started to reflect on the question. It continued to seem odd to her. It appeared to be a question she had not been asked in a long time—and certainly one she hadn't asked herself.

This makes sense. Many of us assume the identities that have been placed upon us without taking the time to question anything. We pay close attention to the words that others use to describe us, and we let them define us. We rarely stop to think if there are other words— more accurate words—that we can muster ourselves.

She started tentatively. "I'm Phoebe," she repeated. "I'm a mother. I'm a daughter, a sister, a friend."

"That's a good start," I said. "How did that feel?"

"Fine, I guess," said Phoebe with a shrug.

"Have you noticed something?" I offered. "The words you have used are conditional on other people."

"What do you mean?"

"Being a mother, or a daughter, or a sister. These are all wonderful and important things," I said. "But they require a relationship between you and others in order to achieve their meaning. I want you to stand on your own two feet and define yourself."

She looked at me blankly. So, I went on.

"If we became friends, and any time we went out socially I introduced you as this person's daughter, or that person's sister, after a while that might get a bit annoying, right? You are your own person. So it's revealing to me that your initial instinct was to define yourself within the context of other people."

I paused, and she sat there silently, so I eased her along with another prompt.

"When you think about being a daughter, or a mother, or a friend, what are some core values that you associate with those roles?

She sat there for a while and didn't offer anything.

"Why don't I give you some words I think describe people who play those roles well," I said. "Kindness, strength, resiliency."

She sat up a bit in her chair, realizing she wanted to pitch in.

"A mother needs to be patient and nurturing, but also firm and protective," she said.

"That's good, go on," I said, excited that we had a dialogue on our hands.

"A good friend is loyal, supportive, and honest," she went on, gathering steam.

She continued with a flurry of adjectives to describe the ideal sister, partner, and employee.

"Okay, let's pause here and reframe things a bit," I said. "You described yourself as a mother, a sister, and a friend. Do you think, all things considered, you are good at fulfilling these roles?"

"Well, yeah, I guess," said Phoebe, obviously uncomfortable at the thought of being self-congratulatory. "I mean, I'm not perfect and I don't always get things right, especially with my kids. But I think I do a good job of taking care of the people in my life and helping them."

"Great, so let's restate what we now know," I said. "Instead of saying 'Phoebe is a mother, a sister, and a friend,' I am going to describe you in a different way, with the vocabulary we have found together. 'Phoebe is nurturing, protective, firm when she needs to be, supportive, loyal and honest.'"

Phoebe's eyes widened, and she looked slightly aghast, seemingly shaken to the core by this simple act of reframing.

"That's a trick; that's not how I describe myself," she eventually said, returning to her usual habit—a habit that so many of us have—of dismissing any chance that she might actually be worth something.

"There's no trick there," I said. "We agreed that you are good at those roles, and we agreed on the attributes required to be good at those roles. I may have pointed you in the right direction, but you found those words yourself, and they describe you perfectly. You are all of those things, and now we simply have to help you see that for yourself."

An authentic identity lay deep within Phoebe, neglected and gathering dust like a once cherished childhood doll now laying long forgotten in the attic. Helping her navigate back to herself would take time, but slowly, she began to describe herself without positioning herself in the service of others.

"I am strong," she said, with a chuckle.

"I know it sounds silly," I said. "But it's the truth. Say it like it's the truth."

"I'm strong," she repeated, this time with more conviction.

With each passing adjective, she grew in confidence, projecting the words with force, demanding that they be heard. She started to believe in them.

"Now I'm going to give you two options," I said. "Option one: I can describe you as a mother, a sister, and a daughter. Option two: I can describe you as nurturing, loyal, honest, and supportive. Which option do you prefer?"

"Option two," Phoebe blurted, surprising herself with how quickly she arrived at her answer.

"I like that option as well." I smiled. "The thing is, lots of people are mothers and daughters and friends. Not everyone embodies the other words that we know describe you. These are your core values; they make you who you are, you have made the choice to embody them, and you should take pride in that."

We wrote down the words we had come up with, sketching out her core values and adding in more vocabulary, striving to fill out an ever-richer depiction of the woman she was.

She spent so much time fulfilling others' needs, but what was it that fulfilled *her*? She bent over backwards to ensure that others wanted for nothing, but what gave *her* satisfaction? What lifted her up; what gave her joy? And when we found answers to those questions, I then asked how much time she spent doing those things.

"I'm going to come full circle now, Phoebe," I said. "Tell me, who are you?"

She took a moment, but this time it was to truly consider her answer; she was no longer confused by the question.

"I am kind. I am caring. And I am joyful," she said with confidence. "These three things are most important to me. These are the three things that are me. They show up in many aspects of my life, and sometimes not as much as I'd like them to, but they're there under the surface. And these are the three things that when they don't show up, I feel uncomfortable within my body and with what I'm doing. It makes me feel agitated and off-balance."

In this session, we had started to identify who Phoebe was at her core, her most authentic self. We noted that expressing these core values made Phoebe fulfilled and at ease. We discussed that there were other traits that she had adopted that did not sit alongside these core values, traits that she had picked up for a multitude of reasons—perhaps they were bad habits, or she felt that they were forced upon her by others, or by society. In any case, these traits made her feel uncomfortable and disoriented. They were not part of her true identity.

For Phoebe, this was a beautiful breakthrough. She had begun to grasp the dynamics of identity and saw that her discomfort came from losing sight of herself. This happens to us all; it's only natural. What is important is finding a way to navigate back to ourselves.

Sometimes we need to break down to break through. We have to reach a crisis point to realize that there is an issue in the first place.

But it is imperative to understand that being uncomfortable inside your own body is not a healthy state, nor should it be a state that you accept. It's a state you're meant to work through, break through, and find your way back from. The natural state of your cells is healthy.

And this journey is ongoing. You are going to change and evolve. Your priorities will shift; what makes you happy and fulfilled will develop over time. You need to ensure that you check in with yourself every now and then and ask yourself the Big Question. You're going to start to understand yourself better and better, and peel back the layers of who you truly are and start to embody your most authentic self.

What I promise you is that when you start this journey—carefully, step by step—you will start to feel more comfortable within yourself. You will start to feel at home when you cultivate this peacefulness, this connection, this relationship with yourself, which is ever-growing and ever-loving.

The stronger that we make this connection to your authentic self, the more comfortable you're going to be in this existence, and the more comfortable you're going to be embodying who you're truly meant to be.

And who you're truly meant to be is a very powerful person. Because when you're operating from a place of confidence and authenticity, success, abundance, and happiness all move within reach.

The first step is to ask yourself the Big Question; don't be afraid of what comes up when you do. Don't shy away from it. Once you do it the first time, you understand that it's not going to crush you.

The sooner you get a firm grasp on your core values—on what makes you the person you are, on your identity—the sooner you can sniff out the parts of your life that you are not living authentically.

If something doesn't feel quite right, it doesn't matter if it's small and trivial, it can still cause discomfort, like a pebble in your shoe. It will sit there digging into your foot with each step, and it will be all you can think about for the entire walk. Of course, what you need to do is take a second to resolve the issue. But I feel like, when it comes to the discomforts in our lives that are connected to identity crises, we simply endure—we don't take the time to remove the pebbles from our shoes, we soldier on and grin and bear it. Even when the discomfort slows us down, we limp along with strained smiles on our faces.

It's time to tap into your intuition. It's time to show up for yourself, constantly, consistently, and compassionately. It takes practice; sometimes we might fall back on past familiar habits that served us for a point in time and maybe don't serve us anymore, and that's perfectly fine. Maintaining strength in identity and authenticity requires ongoing effort.

I will continue to help you along the way, just as I did with Phoebe. The questions I asked her were challenging, and we are going to raise the very same questions, you and I, together. So be gentle with yourself and ensure that you're giving yourself the space that you need to show up wherever you are.

THE VALUES MENU

Whether we realize it or not, we prioritize certain values every time we make a decision. What ten values rise to the top for you? Circle them. What three are the most essential along your path in life? Mark them with a star. This exercise will help you establish your core values and guide you towards leading a more authentic existence.

____ Acceptance	____ Grace	____ Patience
____ Accountability	____ Growth	____ Peace
____ Action	____ Happiness	____ Perseverance
____ Adventure	____ Harmony	____ Recognition
____ Authenticity	____ Honesty	____ Reputation
____ Balance	____ Humor	____ Resilience
____ Beauty	____ Imagination	____ Respect
____ Challenge	____ Independence	____ Responsibility
____ Commitment	____ Individuality	____ Security
____ Community	____ Integrity	____ Self-awareness
____ Compassion	____ Joy	____ Self-reliance
____ Contribution	____ Justice	____ Self-respect
____ Conviction	____ Kindness	____ Service
____ Courage	____ Knowledge	____ Simplicity
____ Creativity	____ Leadership	____ Sincerity
____ Curiosity	____ Learning	____ Spirituality
____ Determination	____ Logic	____ Stability
____ Excellence	____ Love	____ Strength
____ Fairness	____ Loyalty	____ Success
____ Faith	____ Modesty	____ Trustworthiness
____ Friendships	____ Openness	____ Wealth
____ Frugality	____ Optimism	____ Wisdom
____ Fun	____ Organization	
____ Generosity	____ Originality	

Chapter Three

THE STRUGGLE FOR
WOMEN TODAY

I would like to introduce you to Sofi. She's not a real person, more a composite of a multitude of attributes and aspirations shared by modern women. You could say she's a Simulation of the Feminine Ideal (see where she gets her name?).

I'm going to walk you through a typical day in Sofi's life. You might relate to some aspects of her day-to-day routine. You might judge some of the decisions she makes. She might enrage you, or you may empathize with her. Make a note of your reactions; they are all valid, and they will come in handy later on in this chapter.

———

Sofi wakes at 6:00 a.m. Husband lays asleep next to her. She could honestly doze for a good while longer, but she gets out of bed, creeping past Daughter's room and Son's room on her way to the kitchen to make a cup of coffee.

She loves this time of the day. She has half an hour before Husband, Son, and Daughter emerge. Half an hour before she checks her work inbox. Half an hour before she fills school lunch boxes and pet bowls and hungry mouths full of cereal. This time is just for her. Honestly, she doesn't do a whole lot with it. She sips her coffee and looks out across a manicured lawn that borders a pleasant and placid cul-de-sac in Suburban Bliss, USA.

On how many mornings has she looked across this lawn, she wonders? She and Husband moved here from the city six years ago, around the time Daughter started elementary school and Son had just started walking.

Sofi figures she must've looked out on this driveway on at least 1,500 mornings. How many more mornings would she do the same, she wondered? All of a sudden, a knot of dread forms in the pit of her stomach.

"What's for breakfast, Mom?" Daughter says, entering the kitchen, her question shaking Sofi into action.

"I'll make some eggs, and please don't mention Pop-Tarts when your brother gets up because we're not doing sugar in the mornings anymore, okay?"

The rest of the morning is a familiar routine. Husband is up and out quickly—a cup of coffee and a kiss on the forehead—before making his way to work. His office opens a half hour earlier than Sofi's. Somehow this means that he does not contribute to the making and clearing of breakfast, or getting the kids ready, or dropping them off at school. Sofi recalls a distant conversation in which she suggested morning responsibilities could be divided more evenly. Husband praises her for being a "morning person"; meanwhile, he takes "so much longer to get going." The subject has not been revisited, and she can't really figure out why exactly.

Later that morning, Sofi gets on the highway and heads toward the headquarters of Big Brand Inc., where she's worked ever since completing her business studies.

She treasured her time at university and thinks about it often. She fondly remembers getting time to read and debate great literature in a sophomore seminar. She hadn't believed her luck when she discovered a photography course was available each semester. Her parents had always told her that photography was just a hobby that she couldn't pursue seriously. And here she was, honing her skill at capturing the beauty she saw around her, and it all counted toward her undergraduate degree—how lucky was that!

She remembers conversations she'd had with friends from all over the globe. She'd made pacts to visit many of them once she graduated—in India, in Malaysia, in France, in Australia. She hadn't made it out to any of them, of course, but surely there was still time?

She remembers handing out her resume at a stall for Big Brand Inc. during a campus job fair her senior year, and the trepidation that tempered her excitement when she landed an entry position straight out of college. This was all happening so fast, but it would be crazy to pass up this opportunity, right? Thousands of people would have jumped at that offer. She'd quickly moved up the ranks and was soon promoted to Really Important Senior Executive. Her parents were proud of her—she had a generous salary, a great healthcare plan, and a 401K.

Now off the highway, Sofi sits in her car in the parking lot below her office building. A friend of hers had told her once about a special breathing exercise to help get her in the zone before big meetings. Sofi adopted the technique and now runs through the exercise each morning, psyching herself up for the day ahead. It occurs to her that this little ritual she used to enter "boss mode" is very similar to methods for dealing with anxiety and panic attacks.

After all these years, she still feels daunted by the prospect of entering the building. This doesn't necessarily stem from the tasks at hand. Her feelings of imposter syndrome have subsided over time, as she's grown adept and nimble at navigating the many facets of her job description.

Rather, she needs a second to reconfigure herself into a shape that fits neatly within the corporate hierarchy she has to enter each morning. She has a role to play inside this building full of people she spends more time with than her own children. She is responsible for those she manages.

The truth is, her work-life balance is out of whack. Husband has recently started to talk about a third child, and the idea fills Sofi with anxiety. She is already meeting the demands of three needy humans at home, all the while shouldering endless responsibilities and fighting frequent fires at work. The idea of inserting another vulnerable, dependent life into this equation sends her into a panic.

That day, on her lunch break, she leaves the office building and goes to a cafe down the street. She picks at a salad—a collection of leaves, grains, and seeds that all featured in a listicle she once read on "superfoods."

She scrolls mindlessly through Instagram, liking a stream of posts from friends marking kids' birthdays, or new pets, or holidays in Europe, or fancy cocktails, or tasty meals. She hovers over videos from influencers sharing skincare routines and workout tips and fashion advice and recommendations for makeup products and any number of lotions and potions.

She puts the phone down and stares outside of the cafe window onto the busy street, her stomach clenched in a tight ball, refusing to take any more of the tasteless meal in front of her.

Sofi has always loved doing her makeup and finding new outfits to wear. But lately, she's started to feel like she no longer works on her appearance for herself. When did self-expression become performance? When did she stop reflecting her true self-image? She feels like Frankenstein's monster, cobbled together from fashion magazines, social media posts, diet fads, reality TV shows, and gym memberships. She still can't shake a conversation she'd had at dinner a few months ago with Husband and Friend.

"I find it really tough," said Friend. "Ever since I had my kids, there's this section of my wardrobe that I can no longer use. I don't clear it out because I'm hopeful that one day those clothes will fit again, but as each year goes by, I just know it's a battle I'm not going to win. I should be okay with this, it's just a part of my body changing with age and motherhood. But I'm really not okay with it. I hate it."

"You shouldn't feel that way," Husband said with sympathy. "I love the way Sofi's body looks now."

"Excuse me?" Sofi said, her face flushed. "What do you mean by that?"

"I was just saying that Friend shouldn't feel bad about her body changing; it's not necessarily a bad thing," Husband said.

Sofi felt like she'd been punched in the gut. Did he know how hurtful it was to be called out like that? Had he been waiting, biding his time, trying to find a way to work this subject into conversation without looking like an asshole?

Whatever his intention, his comments sent Sofi spiraling. Her insecurities around her changing body were no longer a solo-battle fought within the confines of her own mind. It was now a spectator sport, Husband had front row seats, and he was within his rights to chime in, apparently.

Sofi finishes up for the day at Big Brand Inc. and drives back home. Son and Daughter are on the sofa, tablets in hand, lime-green noise-canceling headphones deafening them to the outside world.

Over dinner, the family plays "rose and thorn," as is tradition. Son is excited about football practice starting up again and doesn't like his new math teacher. Daughter received good marks in a science exam and is still feuding with a friend over something she'd rather not talk about. Husband made a big sale at work and thinks he might need to take his car into the shop for engine trouble.

Sofi goes last but pauses. She grasps for a rose, but there is nothing in reach. She'd settle for a thorn, but she comes up empty. She feels numb, sanitized, like she cannot take joy or sorrow in her day because it doesn't belong to her; it is someone else's story.

"Oh, you know," she finally offers weakly. "Same old, same old. Okay kids, dishes in the sink and then homework."

After dinner, Sofi joins Husband in the garage; he wants to show her what he thinks is wrong with the car.

"I think it might be the spark plug," he says with his head in the engine. "Try the ignition now."

She turns the key, and the engine whirs lazily, chugging along and refusing to fire into action.

"Goddamn it," Husband says, before fiddling about elsewhere beneath the hood. "Go ahead and head inside; this thing is screwed."

On her way out of the garage, Sofi spots a plastic storage container high up on a metal shelf, nestled between some old paint tins and a set of dusty camping chairs.

Standing on tiptoes, she reaches up to retrieve the box and set it down at her feet. She lifts the lid and smiles, staring down at a collection of relics from her college years: a leather-bound booklet containing her diploma she never got around to framing, a collection of concert and festival tickets, a chunky scarf knitted for her by her roommate, and her old Leica camera.

She pops out the camera's SD card and replaces the box on the shelf. Later that night, she sits up in bed, her computer on her lap, scrolling through the old shots.

There's an image of the main square on campus in the late afternoon sunshine; large pillars and archways cast thick rivers of shadow across the courtyard as students make their way to evening seminars.

There's a series Sofi captured of an athlete on the varsity diving team, cutting through the air beneath the ten-meter board, the muscles in his shins straining to keep his toes pointed.

And there is an image of a dear friend, an international student from Malaysia who she'd since lost touch with, sitting cross legged on freshly cut grass, mid-laugh, her face creased with joy. Sofi strains her memory, desperate to recall the long-forgotten joke they shared in that moment, her own face now contorting as tears gather in the corners of her eyes.

———

Finding our place in the world is a struggle. It is not helped by the fact that, as women, we are constantly bombarded by outside stimuli telling us what to do, how to look, or reminding us of all the ways we might be failing.

You'll have noticed that nothing particularly awful happened during the day-in-the-life of Sofi. If anything, she lives a seemingly charmed life: she has kids, a husband, a house, a good job. She has security. Is she allowed to feel unfulfilled? Does she have permission to feel unhappy in this privileged position?

To answer that question, let us look at how the concept of the "ideal woman" has changed over time.

We have evolved from the 1950s-era image of the stay-at-home mother, whose role was to maintain the perfect nest to nurture children and support a bread-winning husband.

The ideal has now morphed, maintaining the above traditional values; however, modern women are expected to pursue careers on top of it all. There is only addition; there has been no subtraction. We are expected to be "super women," capable of maintaining the perfect home while executing on positions of professional responsibility.

Were women encouraged to enter the workplace because men had a collective epiphany over the merits of gender equality? Or is it more that one salary can no longer support a family home? I don't believe it is overly cynical to ponder that question and its ramifications.

In any case, we have come to a point where women are pouring into so many other people's cups—their children's, their partners', their bosses'—without having the chance to replenish their own.

Countless women are struggling to meet the needs of children, partners, and employers, with little time to consider their own needs, much less their dreams and desires.

How can we live authentic lives when we are pressured to fulfill roles that have a predetermined set of characteristics? We are preconditioned to be caregivers from the day we are given our first dolls and toy strollers.

At a young age, we are now told we can be whatever we want to be, as boys always have been, just as long as we don't neglect our domestic responsibilities along the way.

As nurturers, we are the glue that holds the world around us together. We hold space for others and sacrifice our own freedoms. Our authentic selves—our true identities—fall to the wayside as we attempt to balance labels on our heads like stacks of books.

Home ownership, a sensible and stable career path, marriage and two kids by thirty...who authored these checklists, and why are they handed to us all? And why do we feel judged if we fail to conform to them, if we leave the boxes unchecked? What would happen if we tore them up and replaced them with our own narratives, rich in life experiences that bring us joy, a sense of achievement, and belonging?

In my early thirties, I searched my checklist for that terrible word "divorce," and it was nowhere to be seen. This wasn't part of the plan. And it felt like failure.

I felt like I had failed my marriage. I felt like I had failed the people around me. I felt embarrassed. I felt insecure. As I mourned my relationship, I realized that my identity had become so intertwined with my partner, I did not know who I was supposed to be outside of my marriage. Being on my own was disorientating and terrifying.

Each day, I struggled to regulate my nervous system as I tried to show up for my kids, who felt displaced by a move across the country.

And then one day, while sitting alone in my living room, I decided to seek counsel in a trusted mental refuge. I stepped into the gap and listened to myself within the stillness. Before long, the immediate next right action began to materialize before me, like a lighthouse beacon breaking through the fog.

I had been moving through my problems with reactions rather than intentions. My decisions were based on fear, ego, and insecurity. In the gap, I was able to see a path forward selected by my authentic self, not forced upon me by a checklist.

"You know what? This is the best thing for me," I thought.

The pressure placed upon me by preconditioned programming was lifted.

You can do the same. Check in with yourself. In the gap, you can distinguish between decisions informed by societal expectations, and those that are generated by your authentic self.

Ask yourself: "Am I in this situation by choice? Do I feel comfortable? Am I writing this script, or has it been handed to me?"

It might just be time to adopt radical agency. Is life living you, or are you living life? I like to think of it as painting by numbers. You can produce a beautiful piece of art in this way. But do you feel a true, genuine sense of achievement when you have finished? If you have been told what to do through the whole process, is this artwork truly your own creation? It might be time to break out a blank canvas and make your own brave brushstrokes.

Leaving a stable job of twelve years at a large global bank was one of the scariest decisions I ever made. It was also one of the best things I ever did for myself.

When the first thoughts that I might leave my job started to materialize, I pushed them down. It was just silly, frivolous fantasizing, surely. Why would I leave a secure, well-paying position I had worked so hard to attain? I had worked diligently to fill in so many boxes on the checklist, why would I set the whole thing on fire?

I was good at what I did. I knew what I was signing up for each day, how to execute, how to make a success of things. I still felt challenged, and there was room to grow. Like Sofi, there was nothing "wrong" with my life or the position I had found myself in. Except that it didn't feel like my own, true, authentic story.

When I started my own business on the side, it awoke something inside of me. I was no longer painting by numbers. I was no longer conforming to someone else's rules, reading from someone else's script. I was creating something new in the world, something that was entirely of my own making, generated by my true, authentic self.

I could have carried on as things were, with my business as a pet project, a side hustle. But I knew that the half-in half-out approach was not going to work. My business needed my full attention. And when I stepped into the gap, I realized that only fear was holding me back.

I was scared of the unknown, and I was scared of leaving the comfort of a routine that had become second nature to me. We are pattern-seeking creatures, and when something threatens our routine, it can be unsettling.

I became determined to lean into this fear. I had to slowly start getting uncomfortable if I was going to expand my horizons beyond my wildest dreams.

Over a period of six months, I crafted an exit strategy, a plan for leaving my job and going out on my own. I saved what I could, and then I took the leap. I let go of the tethers that were holding me to the shore, and I embarked on this journey.

I took agency over my life, not knowing what was going to happen but believing in myself. I did this because if I hadn't, the regret would've been too heavy to bear. And that wasn't something that I was willing to live with.

I was not going to stay in a comfortable place and conform. No, I was going to break free, and I was going to overcome and figure out what the possibilities could be.

I also knew I might not succeed. But failure is one of the key ingredients of success. I was excited to see what would happen, and it was okay to be afraid.

I reminded myself that the only limits that I was putting on myself were self-imposed. They were subconscious, and often they were things that I had heard, things I had been told by others.

I knew that my story did not need to fit a mold. I did not need to emulate the lives I watched playing out on screens and in social media posts. No, I needed to be myself, and my uniqueness needed to be celebrated. My story was my own. I was the agent of my life. I would release this pressure to conform, and I would step out of my comfort zone. I would do it afraid, but I would do it. And you can too.

Chapter Four

AWARENESS OF THE GAP

The Atlantic Ocean off the northeast coast of the United States has a special energy. The water is powerful, vibrant, and cold. I have vivid memories of visiting the beach as a child growing up on the East Coast. I remember chasing after sand crabs, which burrowed swiftly into the dark sand before I could get my tiny hands on them.

The horizon divided the foggy gray sky from the sparkling green ocean like a perfectly stitched seam. Thick ribbons of kelp waved lazily below the surface of the water, and the heavy, sulfuric scent of the sea filled my nostrils.

I remember gingerly making my way into the water, dancing between pebbles and stones, slick with seaweed. My skin pricked with goose pimples as my feet and legs made contact with the chilly water, and

I would squeal with delight as I plunged forward into the shallow, breaking waves. When I was around waist-height, I would dive straight in, submerging my whole body beneath the surface.

I would beat my legs and take three or four long arm strokes, feeling the resistance of liquid between my fingers, before coming up for long gulps of air.

I return every now and then to those beaches as an adult. I still make sure to go out for a swim, but I enter more slowly, taking my time to adjust to the temperature, savoring the sensation.

It's curious that cold swimming, a life-long love of mine, is seemingly all the rage these days. Influencers and wellness gurus now make careers out of promoting the powers of cold therapy, and numerous celebrities and professional athletes have added cold water plungers and cryo chambers to their home spas.

Proponents claim that frequent exposure to the cold is good for metabolism and helps with inflammation, speeding up the healing process for sore or damaged muscles. For me, the mental benefits from submerging in cold water have always been the most compelling.

Specifically, I believe that cold water helps me connect with the present moment. You feel the water touch your toes, sending shivers up the backs of your legs. You feel that sharp tingling sensation enveloping your body as you slip inside the icy liquid. You are struck by a beautiful awareness of that moment; you are thinking of nothing else as your mind is dominated with the sensation of transitioning to an extreme temperature and the buoyancy of your body floating, weightless in the water.

The present can sometimes feel like an illusion or paradox. The past and future are relatively easy to conceptualize, encompassing everything that has come before, and everything that is yet to occur.

But how can we get our minds around the present? We spend much of our time planning for the future, or remembering the past, but how much of our existence is spent focusing on the moment we are in? It sometimes seems that as quickly as the present arrives, it vanishes into the past.

The paradox of time has occupied the thoughts of philosophers, scientists, and other thinkers for millennia. Aristotle of Ancient Greece grappled with the fleeting nature of the present moment and argued that time cannot have a beginning nor an end. He posited that a period of time must be preceded by a moment before and after, meaning there cannot be a first nor a last moment in time.

In Buddhism, time is said to be cyclical. Our intuition that time occurs in a linear fashion (made up of past, present, and future moments) is simply a mental construct to help us find order in the world and make sense of our experiences. In physics, Einstein's theories suggest that rates of time run differently depending on relative motion, and forces such as gravity can stretch time.

The conscious experience of time is sometimes described as a passage or flow. Along that flow, neuroscientists have found that humans perceive a so-called "psychological present" that usually lasts a few seconds. I like to describe this as the feeling of "nowness."

I believe that it takes practice to focus on the psychological present. The present is so fragile and fleeting. Our minds are constantly switching between moments in time; meanwhile, our attention frequently alternates between different tasks.

Studies have shown that humans are actually bad at multitasking, because our brains are wired to focus on one task at a time. When we think we are multitasking, we are actually rapidly switching focus between tasks, and this often means we end up doing several things more poorly than we would have done if we tackled actions individually and incrementally.

Plunging into cold water serves to overwhelm the senses, and in doing so, declutter the mind. You are forced to focus on the here, the now. The immediate sensation of coldness is all that occupies your brain. That moment in time, that "nowness" comes keenly into focus.

With practice, I learned to tap into the present moment in other situations, away from the water. I'm now able to feel present sitting at my desk, driving in my car, laying on the couch, even when I'm looking at my children while they are eating dinner, observing them silently, in awe of who they are and all that they are going to be.

And often at night, when I wash my face, I will look upon myself in the mirror and experience a similar kind of awe, brought on by an awareness of who I am, everything I have done to this point, and everything I am yet to do.

So, I invite you to put aside some time each day to practice becoming aware of the present moment. Perhaps do it just after you wake up, before the cut and thrust of your day pulls you in a million different directions. Pick a comfy spot to sit and just...be. Focus on the moment, on the present, become aware of that fragile moment in time and cradle it, nurture it in your mind.

This is fantastic training for becoming aware of the gap between your thoughts. Like the present moment, the gap between thoughts is fleeting and ephemeral. Acknowledging it takes focus and awareness.

I referred in an earlier chapter to the relatively new discovery that humans experience, on average, 6,000 thoughts in a day. This figure comes from a 2020 study by researchers at Queen's University in Australia, who used neuroimaging to devise a method to detect where one thought ends and a new one begins.

"We had our breakthrough by giving up on trying to understand what a person is thinking about, and instead focusing on when they have moved on," Jordan Poppenk, the psychologist who led the study, said in a press release. "Our methods help us detect when a person is thinking something new, without regard to what the new thought is. You could say that we've skipped over vocabulary in an effort to understand the punctuation of the language of the mind."

I love the analogy of punctuation as this is exactly my experience of the gap—it acts as the space between two words in a sentence, providing closure for a thought in the past and brimming with the potential of future thought.

Becoming aware of the present is a necessary skill in order to identify this space, this gap between thoughts. So, take a moment. Focus on the present and sit with it. See how it feels to be solely in the moment, present within yourself. You cannot control the past, and you cannot predict the future. The present might be a fleeting, fragile moment, but it is the most real thing you have, it is the one thing you can be certain of.

Take a deep breath and feel the peace wash all around you. Feel your breath filling your lungs, in the same way you would focus on the sensation of cold water enveloping your body while swimming. Feel the air travel through your mouth, down your windpipe, into the tops of your lungs, and then deeper, expanding your diaphragm. Focus intently on that "nowness," that 2-3 second window that our brains identify as the psychological present. You will recognize it when it comes. The feeling of being present is one you will never want to let go of after you've discovered it. There is so much more you can do with this feeling, but for now, just focus on getting there.

I challenge you to try practicing awareness of the present ten times each day. This might sound like a lot, but you will soon find that there are plenty of opportunities throughout the day where you can give it a go. When you wake up, before you go to bed, as you stand in the shower (try running cold water!), just before and after meals, even a few stolen minutes at your desk will do.

I once asked a client how often they sit with themselves.

"Well, what do you mean?" they replied, confused. "Who else would I be sitting with but myself?"

"It's perfectly possible to sit alone while being totally consumed by an action or a stimulus to the point where you are ignoring yourself," I said. "If you have your earphones in and you are listening to a podcast, you are not sitting with yourself—you are in a studio with the hosts chatting about whatever topic that week's episode is on. If you are watching a movie, you are a passive passenger in the journey the characters are on. If you are writing a shopping list, you are visualizing yourself walking down a busy supermarket aisle, picking up milk from the dairy section, and grabbing lemons from the produce aisle."

"I feel like you are asking if I ever just stop living my daily life," my client said.

"It's more that I'm asking you to stop and pay attention to the person that is living that life," I replied. "I'm asking you to check in with yourself, to familiarize yourself with who you are. I want you to make sure that you are living with intention, rather than letting life happen to you."

I instructed my client to put aside a few minutes each day to just sit alone and be. No earphones, no screens, no books or movies, no emails or scrolling, just sit and focus on the simple action of being.

A few days later, I checked in with my client, who appeared energized by this process.

"It took me a while, but I think I'm getting the hang of it," they said. "It's funny how difficult it was initially to spend time without a goal in mind—without anything in the future I was working towards. But, after a while, it clicked. I started to feel present, and it was a wonderful feeling. I feel like I'm in the driver's seat, not just along for the ride. I feel like a human agent that is making decisions and my own choices, rather than just doing what I am supposed to do. I find it really fulfilling."

Let me invite you to sit with yourself. Find somewhere still and quiet. The sounds of nature are just fine, but avoid music or similar distractions. Find a comfortable position and start to take stock of your body. Notice how you feel on the inside, notice how the air envelopes you, feel the pull of gravity on your hips, pulling you toward the ground. Notice how your bones support your frame, giving you structure.

Pay attention to this gift you have been given, a human body and mind. Being who you are is the greatest blessing imaginable.

Close your eyes, if you like, and picture the blood flowing gracefully through your body. Feel your heart contracting, pumping your blood through your major arteries, finding its way into smaller vessels that fan out like beautiful branches, replenishing your cells and muscles with oxygen and nutrients, before returning through long veins on the way back to the heart and lungs.

Then focus on your shoulders, relaxing them, letting them fall away from your ears. Proudly push your chest out, tilt your chin up slightly, straighten your back, and sit up nice and tall, as if an invisible thread attached to your head is being pulled up from the ceiling. Focus on the warmth emanating from the skin on your arms, your hands, your legs and feet.

And now check in with yourself. What do you feel? Are you relaxed and at peace? Is there a tension within your body or in the muscles of your face? Do you feel tired? Do you feel like crying? Is there something you have been holding on to for so long you forgot that you could let it go? Do you feel grateful for being?

When we start to practice awareness, we begin to encounter so many parts of ourselves that we have overlooked, both positive and negative. Becoming aware helps us celebrate the good, rather than taking it for granted, and address the difficult, rather than burying it.

Accessing the present moment in this way will become easier the more you practice. Soon, you will not have to carve out that much time or identify the perfect spot. You will be able to achieve awareness whenever and wherever you need, multiple times a day.

Sitting with yourself can bring peace, liberation, and release. When was the last time you felt these things? When was the last time you stepped inside yourself and became aware of who you truly are? It might feel strange and daunting at first, but this is precisely the preparation we need to undergo before stepping into the gap. You can think of it as stillness or meditation; call it what you like. Just make sure to practice and become familiar with the feeling.

As you encounter those 6,000 thoughts whizzing through your head each day, think about how many of them are focused on the past and the future. I would bet that makes up a large portion. You are worried about making ends meet this month, or that your child might come home from school in tears from bullying or bad grades. You are preoccupied by something hurtful your partner said at dinner last night. You might feel an uncomfortable shiver move through your body with the awkward memory of an embarrassing moment you continue to fixate on, which everyone else has long forgotten.

Our minds are rife with thoughts about the past that we cannot change and worries about the future that we cannot control. We have the opportunity to find peace and groundedness by focusing on the present, yet we rarely take the time to do so.

Those who practice meditation will be well aware of the benefits of sitting with one's self. Some of the earliest references to meditation come from the Vedic religion, which practiced in what is now India between 1500 and 1200 BC. Some historians believe that meditation may have formed part of religious practices dating all the way back to 3000 BC.

Most will be aware of the link between Buddhism and meditation, and the word *meditation* itself might conjure up images of a wise guru, sitting in lotus pose under a fig tree. You may also have misconceptions about the goals of meditation, and this in turn might lead you to believe that you are not doing it right, or worse still, that you can't meditate whatsoever.

Let's take a brief moment to dispel these misconceptions. First, you might think that you have to sit still and in total silence to meditate. To be clear, this does help, which is why I earlier recommended finding a quiet spot when you start out practicing mindfulness and awareness. But once you become familiar with meditation, you can practice it in all sorts of situations, whether it be walking the dog, on a hike through nature, or in the shower after a long day at work.

Another myth of meditation is that you have to reach a state where your mind is totally clear of thoughts. For most people, this state is almost impossible to attain, and that is totally fine. Meditation is not about emptying your mind of thoughts. Rather, it's about becoming aware of the process of thoughts entering and exiting your mind, like clouds across the sky, changing shape and blowing beyond your field of vision. It is about letting these thoughts come into focus, and then passing away, without judgment or attachment. Thoughts can and will occur during meditation—but the meditative state is about letting these thoughts flow through you without fixating on them as you normally would.

Make sure to regularly check in with your body. Allow your breath to anchor you. Your breath is what relaxes you, brings you calm and peace, and returns you from your sympathetic ("fight or flight") nervous system to your parasympathetic ("relax and balance") nervous system.

Here is a simple breathing exercise I encourage my clients to practice. Take a deep breath in, filling up your lungs. Shift from shallow to deep breathing by using your diaphragm and imagine inflating your body like a balloon, letting the air wash through you with its cleansing power. Take air in through your nostrils as deep as you can. Take in a last little bit right at the top. Hold for just a moment, just a second longer than you normally would, and then exhale out of your mouth until every last molecule of air has left your lungs.

If you like, you can introduce a count. Hold at the top for a count of two, then exhale at the bottom for a count of seven. Adjust the timing for whatever's comfortable for you and your body, but always make sure that inhaling and exhaling lasts a little longer than normal. This will return your body to the control of the parasympathetic nervous system and calm you, priming you for a state of self-awareness and letting your body relax.

My partner now uses this breathing exercise when he can't sleep at night and feels like the weight of the world is on his shoulders. Helping him fall asleep is among the greatest gifts I've had the pleasure of offering him.

I even encourage my children to follow this breathing exercise when they are worked up or anxious. Children feel so deeply yet often don't have the vocabulary to express their emotions. Watching children work through their feelings is such a beautiful process— and one I think adults can learn from. We may have the words to express ourselves, but somewhere along the way, we might have lost the ability to let ourselves become vulnerable. We have a hard time saying our feelings out loud. Witnessing a child express a complex emotion for the first time is a truly beautiful moment and always reminds me that we should never take for granted our ability to express ourselves.

Reflecting on childhood and seeing the world through children's eyes can be revelatory. I think too often we overcomplicate things as adults; we lose sight of what it means to be human and what a gift existence is to us all. I believe children are keenly aware of this gift. The joy they find in the simplest things is a reminder of this. When a baby first discovers that they have hands and feet, they can't stop looking at them. They are in awe of what it is to be human, what it is to be alive. We forget that.

We need to tap back into the awareness of what it is to be human, the miracle of what it is to be alive. There is nobody else in the world like you. You are unique in who you are, how you do things, how you say things, and how you think. You just need to become aware of this authenticity.

We will soon see how this awareness can help you shape your future self. But for now, I want you to focus on the present moment. Find that peace, focus on each thought as it passes through your mind, and notice the gap in between.

This is the first building block toward understanding our authentic selves. It is the first step in appreciating and loving ourselves. It will soon allow you to tap into an incredible power and ability to take agency over your life. It will soon allow you to step into the gap.

So, practice accessing the present moment ten times a day. Practice sitting with yourself, taking stock of what it feels like to live within your body. Honor those moments. From there, you will take your first forays into the gap and develop a superpower that will aid you for the rest of your life.

Chapter Five

THE PROCESS OF STEPPING INTO THE GAP

I remember the first time I truly considered the forgotten sixth sense. I was at one of my favorite sushi spots when the waiter brought over my usual order: a dragon roll and a glass of white wine.

This really is a feast for the senses, I thought as I clasped a piece of the roll between chopsticks. It looked stunning: an orange trail of spicy mayo snaked its way across the vibrant green of the thinly sliced avocado. The zesty punch of pickled ginger filled my nostrils; my tastebuds welcomed the rich umami of the soy sauce, along with the sweet flesh of the shrimp. The textures played on my teeth and tongue, crunching through fried batter and squishing soft rice.

It struck me how much of my life was dedicated to seeking out pleasure for my senses of taste, touch, hearing, sight, and smell. But what about proprioception? Why did I not consider this sense in the same way? What would happen if I nurtured this sense with similar enthusiasm and intentionality?

When I began focusing on proprioception—which concerns the sense of where your body is in space—I soon realized it is a vital part of the process of stepping into the gap. Before we step into the gap, we must become keenly aware of where we are in space. This means we have to examine the forces that are acting upon us (such as gravity), as well as the way that our brains and bodies interpret those forces and relay them back to us via our senses.

Proprioception is sometimes called the "forgotten sense" or the "hidden sense" because we tend not to register it or pay close attention to it at all. A lot of the language we use to communicate with one another and describe the world directly stems from what are commonly referred to as "the five human senses": sight, hearing, smell, taste, and touch.

"I hear you," "That sounds good," "That left a sour taste in my mouth," "I feel fantastic," "Something smells

fishy here," "That's touched a nerve," "I see your point"...
the list goes on.

Many of our behaviors are motivated by the pleasures
we draw from these senses: listening to beautiful music,
eating delicious food, getting caressed by someone you
love, watching a stunning sunset, lifting a flower to
your nose.

Perhaps proprioception is not incorporated in the
widely used list of core senses because it doesn't feel like
a feature of our being; rather, it feels like being itself.
Our sense of where we are in space feels more like
our "essence" than it does an aspect of our physiology.
When you describe a tree, you may delineate its roots,
its trunk, its branches, and its leaves...but how do you
describe the space that the tree takes up? How do you
describe the path that the branches take as they grow
toward the light? Those don't feel like attributes; they
feel like the essence of the tree itself, its "tree-ness," if
you will.

To understand the power and importance of
proprioception, it is helpful to consider what it would be
like to live without it. Chances are you know someone
who lives without one of the five senses, or you may be
one of those people yourself. Deafness and blindness
affect millions of people worldwide. Many of us who

contracted coronavirus during the COVID-19 pandemic experienced temporary loss of smell and taste.

People with sensory loss are capable of living rich and fulfilling lives. But what about a loss of proprioception? It is quite hard to imagine living without the awareness of where your body is in space. But there is no doubt that such an affliction would be catastrophic.

A harrowing example of this is explored in the seminal 1985 work *The Man Who Mistook His Wife for a Hat*, in which neurologist Oliver Sacks provides case studies of patients affected by brain disorders. In the chapter "The Disembodied Woman," Sacks recounts the curious case of Christina, a woman who lost her sense of proprioception in the lead up to a routine gallbladder surgery.

A computer programmer and a mother of two, Christina was a healthy and active avid amateur athlete who loved hockey and horse riding. After feeling discomfort in her abdomen, she was diagnosed with gallbladder stones and admitted to a hospital. She was given a dose of preoperative antibiotics and scheduled surgery. She recalled having a dream three nights before her operation where she struggled to stand, felt disoriented, and fell repeatedly.

Bizarrely, when she woke up, her dream came true. She was unsteady, clumsy, and unable to perform routine movements. Her condition deteriorated, and on the day of her surgery, she was unable to stand. Her doctors thought perhaps she was overwhelmed by a hysteria triggered by the expectation of her operation. Sacks was brought in to examine her.

"Something awful's happened," she told Sacks. "I can't feel my body. I feel weird—disembodied."

Sacks found that the majority of her senses were functioning normally, and she could register touch, temperature, and pressure on her skin. He also discovered that she had what appeared to be an almost total loss of proprioception. She had no idea where her limbs and body were located in space. If she was unable to see her finger, or her arm, or her foot, she was not only unable to move the limb or digit; she was unaware of it being there altogether.

After weeks of working with Christina, Sacks eventually helped her regain some form of mobility, which required huge concentration and often a visual connection with the target body part. One afternoon, he showed her footage of herself in a home video, shot before her condition set in. He asked if she recognized the woman in the video.

"Yes, of course that's me," Christina replied. "But I can't identify with that graceful girl anymore! She's gone."

Christina described the feeling of having something "scooped out" of her, as if she had been "pithed." Without an ability to connect with her body—and void of any awareness of her limbs and flesh—her essence, perhaps her very soul, felt diminished.

I provide this example to illustrate the importance of proprioception, and why I think it is problematic that we do not nurture and connect with this sense as avidly as we do others. We endlessly entertain ourselves with visual or auditory stimuli. We crave titillation for our taste buds, or the warm touch of another's skin. I want you to treat proprioception with the same attention that you do your other senses. A good way to do this is by honing in and focusing on the effects of gravity on our bodies.

Follow me in an exercise. Close your eyes and keep still. Focus on the pull of gravity on your body, starting from the crown of your head, down the sides of your face and ears, down your neck, across the tops of your shoulders, down your arms, all the way out through your fingertips, and then, down the side of your body, to your hips. Feel the force of gravity pull down on your legs, your knees, your shins, down to your ankles, to your feet.

The term *proprioception* comes from the latin words *proprius* (one's own) and *perception*. This exercise is a way to perceive your own self, to connect with who you are and what makes you *you*.

Now, take a deep breath, filling your lungs with air. Focusing on slow, deep breaths is proven to create a relaxing effect. When you are at rest, your breathing and heart rate both decrease, as your body is under the control of the parasympathetic nervous system, which is sometimes referred to as the "rest and digest" system.

Conversely, the sympathetic nervous system takes over during periods of activity, overseeing the "fight or flight" response when a threat is detected, including spiked adrenaline, rapid heart rate, and shallow breathing.

Choosing to breathe with deep, slow, intentional breaths has both a psychological and physiological effect on the body, encouraging the parasympathetic nervous system to take over and creating a deep state of relaxation.

Draw a long breath and release yourself from gravity; picture yourself beginning to float, lifting off the ground with a lightness you've never experienced before. The air in your lungs is acting as the thrust beneath a bird's wing, or the swim bladder of a fish, allowing you to ascend through space, uninhibited, free and floating along a beautiful river of air and light.

Release your breath and take another, feeling the air filling the tops, middle, and bottom of your lungs, expanding your diaphragm. You are a cloud lazily gliding through the troposphere; you are an eagle riding thermals, cutting loops through rising columns of warm air.

In this state, we are perfectly prepared to step into the gap. This is how we find ourselves lifted, light, and connected to who we truly are. Not pressed down by the heaviness that comes into our life through trials and challenges.

This is the lightness of the gap. This is what it feels like in your body to be inside the gap, unburdened and free. As we walk through this process, we will start simply by holding onto this feeling of floating in a beautiful, crystal-clear, warm ocean, with a weightlessness to your emotions and freedom from worry.

Now inside the gap, it is time to allow your thoughts to re-enter your mind. Consider whatever worries that brought you to seek out the gap in the first place. Perhaps those worries seem less concerning than at first. Perhaps they've left altogether, or perhaps they have been replaced with new ones, like ships suddenly emerging on the horizon. All of that is totally fine. We've discussed in previous chapters how you have over 6,000 thoughts in a day; each one starts and ends, and there is space between where one ends and a new one begins.

Consider what was concerning you before you picked up this book, pulled out the bookmark, and started this chapter. Think about whatever it was that had you in knots today. Then, as that thought recedes, focus on the space behind it, as you float untethered within the gap. Focus on the idea of that space, the potential of it, the salvation within it, that pause between two great waves.

Before the next wave comes, close your eyes and take a deep breath and feel the lightness in your body. For a split second, there is space—there's the gap—just before your next thought has begun. And then the gap will close, as a new thought tumbles into view. But that millisecond, that ephemeral moment in time, that cognitive vacuum, the space between a period and the beginning of the next sentence...that is where we are going to play.

The ability to open and close your eyes and regulate your breathing helps to mimic the arrival and exit of individual thoughts. As you move from shallow to deep breathing, it helps to count. Breathe in for four seconds—one, two, three, four—then hold for two—one, two—and finally breathe out for six—one, two, three, four, five, six.

Focusing on your breath is a proven way to stop your mind from racing and instead enter a state of relaxation. I believe it also helps to connect us with our authentic selves. Mindful breathing is a central practice in Buddhism, Taoism, and yoga. The word for *spirit* in Ancient Greek is *pneuma*, which translates as "breath"; meanwhile, the English word *respiration* derives from the Latin word *spiritus*, which means both *spirit* and *breathing*. Numerous examples of breathing techniques exist in a range of cultures, including Noho Pū, a traditional Hawaiian breathwork practice and form of meditation, and Senobi, otherwise known as "Japanese long-breathing."

If you prefer not to count, you can instead focus on the breath itself, visualizing the air going into your body through your nostrils, down into your throat, down into the lobes and bronchioles of your lungs, expanding your diaphragm. Think about the space in your body cavity expanding, creating that buoyancy and lightness.

It takes practice to master the process of stepping into the gap and finding your way out of that constant stream of thought. We are endlessly bombarded by our inner dialogue, and it will take time to find that place of calm and poise. But if you try repeatedly, you will get there, and it gets easier and easier.

The gap is there for you during periods of major flux, as much as it is there to rely on when you feel overwhelmed and triggered by seemingly trivial events.

There is a stanza in a Rudyard Kipling poem called *If* that always reminds me of the gap. Kipling wrote the poem as a kind of guide of paternal advice for his son, and it ends in this way:

"If you can fill the unforgiving minute
With sixty seconds' worth of distance run—
Yours is the Earth and everything that's in it,
And—which is more—you'll be a Man, my son!"

Instead of reacting out of frustration or anger, Kipling advises his son to take a beat. Personally, when I feel like those unforgiving minutes are mounting in my own life, I seek out the gap, and it helps me find balance as well as constructive resolutions to my problems.

I remember one day feeling exhausted while driving on a long road trip to visit friends several hours away.

"Honey, please hold your milkshake with both hands," I said to my daughter—I could see in the rearview mirror that she had the drink clasped precariously in one small hand.

"Okay mum," she said without looking up; the kind of response you get from your child where you know the request has been disregarded as quickly as it was received.

I'd been up since 6:00 a.m., but it wasn't just the early rise that made me tired—I was emotionally exhausted. I felt weary in my bones. My recent divorce had left a deep wound in my heart that promised to heal far more slowly than I'd hoped for. I had moved across the state, away from the safety net of family and friends; meanwhile, the kids had started new schools. They were trying their hardest to adapt, though often came back home more subdued than usual. When you become a parent, you share the burden of your children's anxieties along with your own. The pain of my separation was deepened by the guilt I felt for creating unrest in my kids' lives. I had also started a new relationship with a man who had the potential, I felt, to become a great love. But was this the right time? Was it too soon? And was I just setting myself up for more heartbreak?

"Uh oh," my daughter said nervously. I glanced up in the rearview mirror. The leather seats were covered in spilled strawberry milkshake.

"I'm sorry, I'm sorry, I'm sorry," my daughter repeated over and over. I pulled over to inspect the confectionary carnage. The shake had dribbled down from the seats and formed a pool in the footwell. I thought about the clean-up job ahead, and the stink of spoiled dairy emanating from any hard-to-reach crevices I undoubtedly would miss.

I felt blood rush to my face, and my pulse quickened. I wanted to yell or cry; I wasn't sure which. How could she be so careless after I expressly warned her just seconds ago? I could feel the frustration boiling up inside of me—much more frustration than was appropriate to direct toward a child over literal spilled milk.

I took a beat. I closed my eyes and regulated my breathing. Deep breath in (one, two, three, four), hold (one, two), breathe out (one, two, three, four, five, six). I focused on my body, locating my head and each of my limbs in space. I felt the familiar pull of gravity, the weight of my shoulders pulling my collarbones into a slant, the weight of my palms pressing into the steering wheel, my hips pushing onto the car seat, my feet planted reassuringly.

Then I imagined the pull lessening, more and more until I levitated from my seat. I focused on my breathing, and the turmoil of my thoughts retreated from my mind like pylons passing by the window of a speeding train.

I entered the weightless comfort of the gap. I felt centered and at peace. I returned to the moment at hand. I was able to distinguish between "causes" and "triggers." The cause of my frustration and angst in this moment was the pain and feelings of failure surrounding my divorce, as well as the anxiety and uncertainty I felt adjusting to a new life with my children, far away from my familiar support network. My frustration was not *caused* by the spilled milkshake—the milkshake was the *trigger*. It set off a reaction that had been building inside of me for months, which was always going to happen. If it wasn't the milkshake today, it would have been something else tomorrow—a flat tire, an unexpectedly high bill, a careless comment from a friend.

Stepping into the gap allowed me to make this distinction, redirect my negativity, and approach the problem with a more constructive attitude. The trigger of the spilled milkshake revealed that there was a lot of unaddressed angst within me. If I did not take the time to resolve these troubling emotions in a controlled manner, they would not stay buried—rather, they would spill out in a chaotic fashion. In that short moment inside the gap—mere seconds—I was able to distinguish between the cause of my pain and the triggers for my outbursts. And I knew I had a choice between control and chaos.

Before, there'd been a maelstrom of emotions, each competing to win out—like in the Disney movie *Inside Out*. After my time in the gap, I realized I could feel all of these emotions keenly, but I had the choice not to allow them to dictate my actions.

"It's okay, honey, it was just an accident," I said to my daughter. "We'll get it cleaned up when we get home."

And you know what? I was proud of my reaction. I thought, *Wow, go you!* That might sound silly—no one should really expect accolades for not lashing out. And it was just a spilled shake. But anyone who has had an argument with a loved one will be able to relate that, very often, you're not really arguing about the trigger. You are arguing about much, much more.

In the example of a boyfriend and girlfriend yelling at each other over unwashed dishes in the kitchen sink, the outpouring of emotion is not about that particular load of dirty plates. It's likely about a larger, more systemic imbalance in the relationship.

The way we make other people feel correlates to our own wellbeing. Overreacting to triggers can cause lasting harm to our relationships, and in turn, add feelings of guilt, remorse, and regret to your own bubbling cauldron of negative emotions.

Sitting in the car with my daughter, I either wanted to yell or leave the situation entirely. Just get out of the car and walk away. I was tired; I was impatient. I was operating from a place of physical and emotional exhaustion. But a brief spell in the gap helped me to choose control over chaos and come to a deeper understanding of what I was feeling. Not only had I not overreacted in that moment—I now knew it was imperative that I tended to myself and addressed the causes of my pain, so as to avoid taking it all out on loved ones and deepening my state of disquiet.

I hope this example helps you see that you can practice entering the gap in pretty much any situation. You do not need to reserve the technique solely for traumatic moments. The gap can help you navigate seemingly trivial bumps along the road. This is especially important, since trivialities can act as triggers for outbursts connected to deeper, more painful issues we are yet to resolve.

Embrace the levity within the gap, feel its lightness all around you. You have pressed pause on the moment; you are a cursor on the keyboard, blinking with anticipation for the words you are yet to write. You are going to decide what comes next with real intention. You are not going to let what has come before dictate what comes next. You have true agency.

A client of mine once described how crippling doubt was discouraging her from taking on new challenges and truly pushing herself.

"It's so difficult," she said. "I spend so much time building up to a big decision. I try to encourage myself to take action and take a leap. I know what I am doing right now is not working, and I need to have courage and make a real go of things. But just before I jump, my doubt stops me. I want to take it all back. I can't do the thing. I can't push myself that far. I am not capable of it."

This dynamic will surely sound familiar to most. Procrastination, inaction, and maintaining an unfulfilling status quo are all a form of self-sabotage brought on by fear of the unknown. And sometimes, it's more than that.

I spoke with my client about entering the gap, right in that moment before the doubt creeps in.

"As soon as you have built up the confidence to take a big leap, that's when I want you to pause and enter the gap," I told her. "I want you to enter the space before your courage subsides to self-doubt. This is where you will be able to find out what is truly holding you back."

We practiced going through the steps of entering the gap several times.

"There's nothing else there right now," I told her. "It's just space. It's just lightness. It's just levity. Feel how good that feels in your core. There's no tension, no pressure. I want you to repeat the word 'yes, yes, yes, yes'. Sit in this space for as long as you can. This might be difficult at first, and the doubt might creep in like dark clouds and block out the sunshine of your positive affirmation. But with practice, the light will begin to break through and eventually burn away those clouds, turning them to vapor and enveloping you in a warm glow."

My client grew in confidence and soon began to feel that levity, that beautiful weightlessness of the gap. After using the exercises we worked on in her own time, the next time we met, she was buzzing with the excitement that comes with personal revelation.

"I think I've figured it out," she said. "I was in the gap, and things became so clear to me. It wasn't fear that was holding me back. It wasn't really the unknown. I realized it was I suspected that I would fail. And if I tried, I would confirm those suspicions. If I didn't try, then I would just avoid the possibility of failure altogether."

"That's a wonderful, powerful insight," I said. "You can't avoid failures in your life. You must embrace them. Confidence doesn't come from success. Confidence comes from overcoming failure. What do you think you'll do now?"

"Well, I now have a reason behind my hesitation," she said. "I now know I need to work on accepting the possibility of failure. I have a lot more work to do, but I'm kind of excited to do that work; now I have the gap to help me along the way."

I particularly like this example, because it shows how the gap is part of an ongoing process of self-improvement. It is not a cure-all; that doesn't exist. When you resolve an issue or come to a realization in the gap, you will often realize there are further obstacles in front of you. That is how life works. But the gap will give you the confidence and the tools to overcome those obstacles, instead of giving in to them.

My client was now one step closer to approaching her life with agency, intention, and action, instead of doubt, uncertainty, and inaction. A battle between her positive incantation—"yes, yes, yes"—and creeping doubt was played out within the gap, and the former came out victorious. She had evolved. She had stepped out of her comfort zone and realized what she was truly capable of.

Now that we have explored the methodology behind entering the gap, I'd like to invite you to practice the process. A great place to start is each morning, when you wake up and are laying in bed. Before you get up and start your morning routine; before you get changed and make your coffee; before you fully open your eyes and embrace the day; before you start to feel that first thought creep in, whatever it might be, spend some time in the stillness.

Take a deep breath and fill your lungs. Bring the oxygen into your body. Feel yourself expand. Pause for a moment and slip into the gap, into the stillness. Drink in that last little bit of peacefulness that comes with sleep. Cultivate that peacefulness in these waking moments, nurture it, hold on to it a little bit longer.

Practice what it feels like just to sit in that space. Do it as often as you need, at any time throughout the day. The more that you do it, the more and more you'll cultivate the lightness, the levity, the lift, the peacefulness that the gap can offer you. Soon, we will start to play within that space and expand it; you'll start to understand more and more what it is to operate with intentional action, to know who you really are, and to be your authentic self. It is a beautiful feeling. So enjoy it. Do it as much as you need to. Recharge that battery, apologize less, and live more.

Chapter Six

EXPANDING THE MOMENT

Mothers know straight away when its nap time for a child. During my daughter's third birthday, I remember seeing the sure signs in her demeanor. I scooped her up. "Time for a nap," I said, planting a kiss on her hot cheek.

"Oh, she's doing just fine," one of my friends protested. "She doesn't want to miss out on her party!"

She was having a blast, of course, playing on the lawn with her friends, chasing fat, iridescent bubbles emanating from the bubble machine. But I could read the signs, sure enough. Her squeals of joy had changed slightly in tone; there was now a tinge of frustration and anguish in her tiny voice. She paused more frequently—she was watching her pals instead of running with them, and she'd raised a chubby little fist up to rub her eyes.

"Trust me," I said, "This party girl needs some downtime. She'll be back before you know it, and we'll cut the cake."

I carried my daughter up to her bedroom, her head now resting on my shoulder, her thumb planted firmly in her mouth. I remember thinking, "Sometimes I feel this way." Sometimes I feel the need to be scooped up and carried off to a place of quiet and stillness. Surely we all do. So why did we stop listening to this need? Why do we feel we must push on through the day in such a relentless manner? Have we forgotten to listen to our bodies? Why do we deny ourselves these moments in the day to pause, take stock, and recover?

Does adulthood mean we forgo the luxury of that "stillness"? Do we "grow out" of the need for nap time? It is worth pondering that going to bed just once in a day is likely a modern habit that differs from sleeping patterns humans exhibited for millennia.

In his book *Sleep We Have Lost: Pre-Industrial Slumber in the British Isles*, historian Roger Ekirch tells us that, prior to the industrial revolution, Britons followed a segmented or biphasic sleep pattern. It was common, Ekirch wrote, for people to go to bed between 9:00 p.m. and 10:00 p.m. for "first sleep," which lasted around three to three-and-a-half hours, before rising for a couple hours to take part in any number of activities—from cleaning and cooking, to reading and socializing. Then people would head back to bed for "second sleep" before getting up again around dawn.

Ekirch writes that, at the time, many parts of the world had this sleeping pattern, including the United States. Biphasic and even polyphasic sleep were likely common even further back in human history, according to multiple references in medieval texts as well as in Homer's *Odyssey*, written in the eight century BC, and Virgil's *Aeneid*, written in the first century BC.

It's likely that better illumination triggered the transition to monophasic sleep around the time of the Industrial Revolution, when powerful oil lamps—and eventually, electricity—became ubiquitous. The 9:00 a.m.–5:00 p.m. workday became popular in the US and Europe in the 1920s, adding a new rigidity to our schedules, and we have never really looked back.

Spain might provide the most well-known example of biphasic sleep persisting in society, but even there, the habit is becoming increasingly rare, with just 18 percent of today's Spaniards regularly taking *siestas*, predominantly in more rural areas.

Learning all of this made me wonder: When we deny ourselves downtime, might this be messing with the way we are wired? Are we refusing ourselves an innate and ancient need for reprieve and stillness?

I believe we need to listen to our bodies and take care of ourselves, just as our parents did when they scooped us up and carried us off for nap time. And don't get me wrong—I'm not suggesting that we all start taking naps in the middle of the workday (though they might be onto something in Japan, where napping at work, or *inemuri,* is commonplace and even encouraged). For many of us, carving out time for napping is impractical or infeasible.

But there are other ways that we can provide ourselves with downtime and stillness. And it is imperative that we explore these ways together, because embracing stillness is a prerequisite for stepping into the gap.

Stillness helps us connect to our authentic selves. It reduces stress, soothes our nerves, and helps us gain perspective. It returns us to a state of balance.

I worked in high-level corporate jobs for twelve years, and I was out of whack that whole time. When I look back on that version of myself, it conjures up the image of a woman balancing a bowl in each hand with outstretched arms, in the form of a human-weighing scale. Except she doesn't have two arms extending from her torso—she holds multiple bowls with multiple arms, like an octopus or the Hindu god Shiva.

Each bowl represents an aspect of her life in which she may pour energy—her job, motherhood, her relationship with her partner, her friendships, her love life, her relationship with herself, her hobbies and pursuits.

Every time she pours energy into a bowl, it nourishes that part of her life. But here's the catch—there is a finite amount of energy distributed across the bowls, and to fill one, she must take from another. Each time she does so, her body cranes slightly toward the bowls that bear the most energy, and away from those that have been depleted. She is most at ease when the energy is approaching even distribution across the bowls, allowing balance and centeredness. She knows that complete balance is improbable—at any time, one area of her life will always require more nourishment than another.

But she also knows that some parts of her life have a ravenous appetite; they will drink deeply from their bowls and demand more and more and more. I can see her now, during that twelve-year period, frantically ladling energy into the bowl for her boss, the bowl for her colleagues, the bowl for her clients, the bowl for her meetings and phone calls and early morning rises and commutes. She was stealing from the bowls for her children, and her hobbies, and her husband, and her family. More and more, she depleted these bowls to fill those that fueled her work, until her body was twisted and contorted, struggling to remain upright under the unwieldy imbalance she had created. She teetered on the edge of disaster, always seconds away from collapsing, sending her precious cups clattering across the floor away from her broken body.

I lived and breathed corporate America. My career thrived because I was motivated and my work ethic unquestionable. But my sources of motivation? You could question those. I was constantly striving to prove myself to others. To prove that I was capable, and that I deserved to be there. This was especially true after I returned twice from maternity leave. Sometimes I felt like taking leave was a burden on the company. I felt guilty for time away, and when I came back, I felt I had to work extra hard to justify my place.

Asking for help felt like acknowledging I was incapable of something. I accepted more and more responsibility, to showcase how much I could do and how much I could bear.

"Look at me over here," I was screaming. "I can do all of these things, and I can get it done quicker, faster than before."

I had to prove that I was as capable, if not more capable, than everybody else. I never gave myself a moment to pause, to do things at my own pace, to cultivate balance in my life—which in the long run would provide more stability and better results. It was go, go, go, for over a decade. The imbalance from filling all those bowls began to manifest itself as pain in my neck and shoulders.

My body was telling me to cultivate stillness in my life; it was pleading with me to slow down. But I didn't listen. I'd forgotten what peace felt like. I didn't identify stillness as a positive—it felt like the opposite. Stillness was laziness; stillness was neglect. I always needed to be doing something, to satisfy someone.

But this is where we need to make a distinction. There is a type of inactivity that can be harmful. Perhaps you've had those moments where the world feels overwhelming, and you need to go to ground. You crawl up in bed and binge Netflix for two days straight. You eat junk food and don't wash your dishes. You don't shower or clean your house or call your friends.

This type of hedonistic and disordered state gave rise to the term "goblin mode," and while it may have its place from time to time, you run the risk of feeding self-doubt and even self-loathing if you indulge it too often. Let's be clear: even though it feels like you are "doing nothing" when in goblin mode, that's never really the case. As long as you are watching a screen, you are distracted, and you are not being mindful.

Stillness requires thoughtful and intentional inactivity. No doomscrolling, no streaming, no distractions. There is nothing lazy about entering true stillness. It takes practice and a certain amount of discipline to truly allow yourself to "do nothing" except be with your thoughts, even for a few seconds. Stillness is a mental state in which you consciously and peacefully analyze your feelings and the causes of these feelings. In doing so, you are taking agency over your life and how you respond to its many pressures.

I like to consider the phrase, "She couldn't see the woods for the trees." That is sometimes how life can feel if you are constantly active and overstimulated. You are moving through the woods at breakneck pace, so fast you can't locate yourself, and you are so distracted by all that is whirring by you that you can't see the bigger picture.

Stillness allows you to zoom out and capture a fuller view. You see the woods in all their beautiful holistic harmony, you see the canopy and the meadows, you see the streams that run through the glens like silver veins, you hear the birdsong and the rustle of fallen leaves upon the forest floor. You become aware of the threads of fungal mycelium that connect the plants and trees in a great network, disseminating nutrients far and wide.

This is your life, and now you have stopped rushing through it; you can view it for what it really is. You can see the parts of the forest that are lush, vibrant and thriving. You can see regions where the plants are wilting and the land is barren. You understand which areas need nurture, and where fires must be extinguished.

Sometimes, we convince ourselves that simply "doing more," "working faster," and connecting ever more frequently to information sources is the answer to our problems. But more often than not, this serves to compound our issues. You might be picking up the pace through the woods; however, a lost sprinter is still lost. And every time they change direction, the way back becomes more confusing. If you stop, stand still, and zoom out to take in the bigger picture, you can see clearly where you are and where your next steps should take you.

When I do this, I feel a sense of relief, elation, lightness, even liberation. And I want you to feel these same things. I want you to call into your life this sense of calm via the self-controlled practice of stillness.

As we live our lives and confront the pressures we all experience, stillness gives us the chance to face things consciously, authentically, and with a state of peace that we can call upon anytime, even in our darkest moments.

Entering a moment of stillness lays the groundwork for entering the gap. If the gap is the moment between thoughts, you can think of stillness as the moment between actions. That is what we are attempting to cultivate.

And this stillness can be both physical and conceptual. First, just stop moving. Sit in a chair or lay on your bed and let your arms and shoulders relax. Detach what you are usually tethered to—your phone, your TV, and your computer. Live in the quiet; expand in the moment.

Recharge and re-energize yourself within these moments of calm. Imagine yourself floating in water, with your buoyant body defying the gravity that works so often to pull us down. I keep returning to water imagery perhaps because I'm a water sign and a beach baby at heart. Though, it might be deeper than that. Water truly bonds us all—it is life-giving and makes up around 60 percent of our body composition. Imagine the molecules of water in your cells bonding with those in the water you are submerged in, eliminating the barrier of your skin so you can no longer tell where your body starts and the water begins. The water is holding you; it's scooping you up like that parent at naptime. You are buoyant, light, and still.

Take in deep breaths and follow the breathing exercises we have covered in previous chapters. You have cultivated this stillness. You have made the decision to stop. You have taken control. How powerful is that? You have taken back the reins on this wild ride, and you have said: "No, I'm going to pause for a moment, and I'm going to think about this. I'm going to take a moment for myself."

Practicing stillness is a key ingredient in the recipe for success. Taking a moment for yourself brings back balance and opens up clear and logical paths forward. These moments of stillness can be long—for example, during hours of meditation at a wellness retreat. They can be short and last just a few minutes: laying in your bed or sitting on your sofa at home. And they can even go by in a flash—just a few seconds of quiet recentering.

I first realized how useful these ultras-swift moments of stillness can be when I observed a director within the bank I used to work for, who I looked up to immensely. She was dynamic, had strong convictions and values; she led her team with efficiency, poise, and grace, and she was a wonderful motivator. All things I tried to emulate and still do.

She occasionally delivered talks, either to the team during fireside chats or to large audiences during keynotes at corporate events. When she fielded questions, I noticed something intriguing. Before she answered, she paused, sometimes for a few seconds. Just long enough for it to be noticeable.

Was she thinking about the answer? Was she choosing her words carefully? Maybe, but it seemed like something different. Usually when people are contemplating an answer, there are some tells or signals. They might look up, as if visually locating an answer from the ether. They might mutter a contemplative and brief "hmm" or buy time with a few "ums" or "uhs." They might say, "That's a great question," or "No one has ever asked me that," indicating they need a brief moment to arrive at a conclusion that hasn't come to them readily.

But this was different. There were no "ums" or "uhs." Her eyes remained centered on whomever directed the question at her. There were none of the usual tells of someone searching for answers.

And then it hit me...she was checking in with herself. She was taking a moment to listen, to center herself, to slow down and ensure that what came next was deliberate and clear-minded. She knew, from experience, that conversations can become complex and unwieldy if we approach them at a reckless pace. Points can be missed. If we don't take the time to find calm and balance and reach a true understanding of a point of view, we can talk at, or beyond, or through someone, rather than with them.

She would pause because she wanted to take agency over how she was going to respond, what she was going to put back out into the world. She cultivated a moment of stillness in order to ensure that it was her true and authentic self delivering the message she wanted to get across.

This pause before speaking is a rarer habit than you might expect. Watch out for it next time you are with a group of people taking part in a debate. I would wager that for every one person that pauses before speaking, there are ten that interrupt each other. Sometimes, it is obvious that a person is not even listening; they are instead formulating what they are going to say next, locking it in the chamber and releasing it with an interjection, elbowing their way into the discourse with a "Yeah, but" or a "Well, actually." Without a moment of stillness, they cannot see the "woods" of the conversation; they are tangled and lost in the "trees" of their own words.

Sometimes, a pause before you speak will allow you to properly take on board the gravity of an individual's words. I recently met a woman for the first time who gave me a great and profound insight into the mind-body connection.

I paused after what she said, allowing the words to solidify in my mind and take root. She looked at me slightly quizzically, since my pause had broken the cadence of conversation that most of us have grown accustomed to.

"I just wanted to take that in," I said. "What a beautiful thing to say."

I have now adopted the habit of pausing in these kinds of moments and others. I do it with my partner and with my children. Finding stillness in conversation leads to greater understandings of ourselves and each other. It makes me smile every time I see others using this practice.

Pausing before you speak is especially helpful in times of high stress. The tried and tested "breathe and count to ten" exercise really does work. It gives us that moment of stillness, which opens up the big picture and realigns us with our parasympathetic nervous system.

If taking pauses before you speak sounds awkward, or sitting with your own thoughts makes you uncomfortable, that's perfectly natural. Uncomfortable is good. Embrace it. *Uncomfortable* is not a bad word. Change is uncomfortable, and if you are reading these pages, it's very likely that change is what you are after. The status quo isn't working, so it's time to leave your comfort zone.

If something makes me feel uncomfortable, I find writing about it to be a helpful exercise. The process of writing things down helps us clarify how we feel and where those feelings are coming from, which in turn allows us to find the right answers.

So, this week, I invite you on each day to find some moments for stillness, then write about your experience after. What conditions did you establish for your moment of stillness? Could they be improved? Did you manage to truly detach yourself? How did the stillness make you feel? Were you calm? Were you anxious? If so, where did that anxiety come from? This kind of reflection will lead you toward a truly examined life, which, as Socrates told us, is the one worth living.

Be kind to yourself. Give yourself these moments of stillness. We have to take care of ourselves, as our parents took care of us. We have to call that support back into our lives.

Children receive care, as do elderly people. In his play *As You Like It*, William Shakespeare describes extreme old age as the "second childhood," with its return to a state of dependency and vulnerability. In the middle stages of our lives, where we are busiest and seemingly independent, we can too readily forget that our need for care and attention doesn't disappear. It is there; we just choose to ignore it. We need to take the time to be still, access the parts of us that need nurturing, and practice self-care.

In this stillness, you will begin to notice the gap between thoughts more readily, and you will be well-positioned to step into it. You will float within a beautiful awareness and authenticity. You can check in with yourself, as well as understand the roots of both pleasure and pain. You are taking care of yourself, and that is among the most beautiful forms of love that exist.

Chapter Seven

YOUR SELF
WITHIN THE GAP

"Do you feel safe?" I asked my friend, who we'll call Peggy, as we sipped glasses of wine on her balcony.

"Well, no, but...I don't know, what does that even feel like?" she said.

"When he calls you, or when he knocks on your door, do you smile, or do you have an uneasy feeling in your stomach?"

"Uh...both, maybe?" Peggy said. "It's like that feeling I had when I was in middle school and my mom was driving me to a house party. Like, excited about the evening ahead, but super self-conscious about my outfit and my hair and nervous I might do or say something stupid."

Peggy was having trouble with a guy she was dating, let's call him Sean. They had been seeing each other on and off for a year now. At first, things went great. They met online and were pretty much inseparable from their first date. After a few weeks, Peggy introduced Sean to her friends, including me, and he was charming, talkative, and showed Peggy a ton of affection.

Things went along swimmingly for the subsequent six months, around which point they went on vacation together to Cabo. One day, they were lounging around the pool, soaking up the Mexican sunshine and drinking mezcal margaritas. They got chatting to another couple, and Peggy introduced herself.

"I'm Peggy, and this is my boyfriend Sean," she said, offering a handshake. They chatted for a while with the other holidaymakers about their plans for the rest of the week and their lives back home, then decided to head back to the hotel room to get ready for dinner.

Peggy told me that, on the walk back to their room, Sean was acting strangely. He was practically silent, offering no input about where they might eat that evening and generally behaving as if a dark cloud had descended on his mind.

Peggy said he was like that for the rest of the trip. She could barely extract full sentences out of him, and when she asked him what was going on, it was the same reply: "Nothing."

When they got back to the United States, after they made their ways to their respective apartments, she didn't hear from him for three days.

He eventually responded, and they agreed to meet up for a talk. It transpired that Peggy's major error was using the term *boyfriend* for the first time. They hadn't discussed their status together, and it had blindsided him; he wasn't sure if they were "there yet," and meanwhile, she had made the decision for him. He thought maybe it was best if they "cooled things off" for a bit.

Peggy called me up after their talk. She was upset and confused.

"I mean, come on?" she said over the phone, her voice wavering. "Look, I know we hadn't had the conversation about being exclusive, and maybe that's my bad. But things had just developed so naturally that it didn't feel necessary. We've been spending more nights together than not for the last six months. We leave stuff at each other's places; we hang out with each other's friends. We booked a holiday to Mexico together! Am I really that crazy for assuming that we were boyfriend and girlfriend?"

A week later he called her and asked if he could come round. He was sorry, he didn't realize what he had until he pushed her away. He was in love with her. He could see that now. Please forgive him. Peggy was elated. They started seeing each other again and got back into their regular pattern—dinners, parties, walks in the park, sleepovers.

Then Sean's words dried up again, and the cloud descended on his mind once more. This was too much pressure, he said. He was not in the right place for this. Was he even capable of love, he wondered?

They went back and forth like this for months— Sean would sweep her off her feet and then withdraw, leaving Peggy reeling with emotional whiplash.

That day on the balcony, I had come over to discuss the latest of Sean's disappearing acts. He hadn't responded to messages for two days, and I could tell my friend was at a breaking point. To the objective observer, the solution was clear: Sean was bad news. He was likely stringing her along and seeing other people. At best, he was emotionally incompetent and not ready for a relationship. She needed to delete his number and never see him again. But I knew that matters of the heart are sensitive, and going in hard would likely force

Peggy to put walls up. I needed to help her come to the right conclusion on her own, rather than force the issue.

"Those two reactions when he calls—your smile and the uneasy feeling in your stomach—they are coming from twin aspects of your being," I said. "I call them 'ego' and 'intuition.' They both make up who you are. They are two inner voices: different, yet connected, like two sides of the same coin. I think you need to analyze what each one is saying to you, and that might help you come up with a path forward."

The ego, I explained, focuses on fear, threats, others' perceptions of us, and above all, survival. Don't think of it in the more common way people talk about ego—as if it's synonymous with arrogance ("his ego entered the room before he did"). Ego can of course sometimes cause negative reactions, but its ultimate goal is to preserve your feelings and protect you from immediate pain.

I told Peggy: "When Sean calls you or knocks on the door, your ego pops up and says: 'We like this guy. He's made us feel good before. We like to feel good. Let's give him what he wants, because if we don't, he might leave us, and if he leaves us, we will be sad and embarrassed, especially because all our friends will say I told you so.'"

Her ego was arguing that, while things might not be perfect, things could get so much worse if she left Sean. There would be no more sleepovers, no more fun dates, no more of the dopamine hits that come with feeling wanted and desired. Should she really risk all of that because he was a bit indecisive? Surely, she should preserve what she had and stay where she was, her ego was saying, instead of heading into the great unknown.

Her intuition, meanwhile, was chiming in with a different story.

"Your intuition is your gut feeling," I told her. "Right now, it is telling you that something is not right. Something's off about this situation that urgently needs addressing. And the thing about intuition is that it is never wrong. I'm not saying you have to act on it. But I am telling you that you need to at least listen. Your ego and your intuition will often voice their offerings at the same time, and this results in a bit of a garbled message. You need to sit in your stillness, step into yourself, and find a way to hear what both voices are telling you with great clarity."

Peggy did eventually end up leaving Sean, but not before enduring a few more rounds of heartache. Her inner voices of ego and intuition continued to pipe up at the same time, clouding and confusing her mind.

I believe it is important to listen to both of these voices. They both have value and can help guide us. But it's essential that we develop the skill of distinguishing between them, so we can move forward with clarity and confidence.

Ego is a part of us that's tied to survival. It is calculating all the things that could possibly go wrong, informed by a deep memory of all the things that have gone wrong in the past. Your ego is most concerned with keeping you safe. It's not necessarily interested in personal growth, which is often contingent on taking risks. It is important to listen to your ego, but you should question whether or not you act on its advice.

We need that part of us. We need to be cautious and experience doubt. A life without fear would likely end in tragedy, as would one without a recollection of previous hardships.

"Remember what happened last time?" your ego tells you. "This scares us. This is uncomfortable; we don't like it."

Your ego can hold you back. It can convince you that enduring the pain of the moment is worthwhile, since the pain of the unknown may be greater. This is a big contributor to people staying in toxic relationships. Your ego is telling you that you don't know what could happen out there. It could be scary. Something terrible could happen.

And the more trauma you experience in life, the louder your ego becomes. In his seminal work *The Body Keeps the Score*, psychiatrist Bessel van der Kolk described soldiers who returned from the Vietnam War and lost the ability to feel love towards their girlfriends or wives after witnessing the deaths of friends in battle. The ego, in this case, told these men to shut down, because the last time they opened their hearts to someone, they experienced devastating loss and trauma.

The ego is like an insurance provider, constantly calculating risk based on historical data. The more wrecks you have been a part of, the higher the premium you must pay in order to take the car back on the road.

And the ego is very happy for us to maintain the status quo, even if it's not quite working for us. Perhaps you are in an environment that is not conducive to personal growth or the expansion of wellness and peace. You have begun considering a change. Maybe you want to explore a new career or move to a new area. You are a fish with its growth stunted by a small tank, and you know it's time for an upgrade.

Meanwhile, your ego is telling you, "No, don't bother. We know this routine. We know this job and this city. It's familiar. It might be a little uncomfortable, but we can bear it. It'll probably be more uncomfortable over there, so there's no point."

But there is a point. Life is full of unknowns, and risks are part of living. We only grow through taking risks and overcoming failure. Sometimes, you need to say, "Thank you, ego; I hear what you are saying. I am going to go ahead and take this risk. Because of you, I am aware of the things that can go wrong, and I am not going in blindly. You have helped me prepare, and now it's time to act."

And that is the key. I am not advising you to ignore your ego. It's smart, experienced, knows you well, and has your best interests at heart. I am instead suggesting that you allow your ego to *prepare* for the leap, rather than letting it *prevent* you from taking the leap at all.

With the advice from your ego in hand, you are able to proceed with a healthy amount of caution. Perhaps instead of leaping headfirst, you dip your toe in the water first. Maybe you'll update your resume. Maybe you'll research the companies you are considering applying to and check online resources with reviews from past employees. Maybe you'll spend a few days in the town you are considering moving to and look for temporary accommodation instead of committing to a long-term lease off the bat. Your ego is a dear friend who doesn't want you to fail. But failure is a core ingredient to success, and we have to stumble and fall sometimes to learn.

Understanding that it is perfectly acceptable to disregard the advice from your ego can be a revelation for those people who have let the ego take the reins. Operating purely from the ego can promote overactivity of negative emotions, including worry, stress, anxiety, and anger.

Oftentimes if we operate from a place where our ego is dictating our actions, our behavior can become counterproductive and even harmful. Van der Kolk described how the Vietnam vets were mostly passive, but when someone told them something disappointing, they could overreact and become frustrated. Negative feelings can often remind us of how we felt during previous traumas and trigger a disproportionate response, in which we lash out or withdraw. Our "flight or fight" response can be activated by a situation that is trivial, because it reminds us of a greater pain.

Feelings build up, and your ego has an immaculate memory. It can be something minor that breaks the dam, allowing your fear and rage to crash through. We've all been there—having an argument with a partner in which our emotions and words are totally disproportionate to whatever it was that set us off. Your partner is standing there, bemused that a towel on the floor is eliciting such a strong reaction. Meanwhile, you are unloading all the ill-will you have built up from numerous other, more substantial examples of inconsiderate behavior that made you feel undervalued and unloved and unwanted.

Uncoupling your actions from your ego—allowing it to guide rather than control you—will help you approach stressful situations from a place of clarity and calm, from your parasympathetic rather than sympathetic nervous system.

You'll then be able to get to the bottom of why something upsets you. "Oh, wow," you might say to yourself, "I feel I am on the edge of overreacting to this stressor. Perhaps it's linked to a past trauma that I'm yet to resolve. I need to spend some time identifying and addressing this trauma, and lessen its influences on my behavior in the present."

Things that need to be seen are going to continue to niggle at you until you address them. And they will often rear their heads at inopportune moments or at times that have a major impact: in the workplace, in our relationships, with our kids and loved ones.

So, step into the gap and begin a dialogue with your ego. Start a conversation and stop taking orders. This dialogue is a process of rest (finding your stillness) and review (checking in with yourself and analyzing your thoughts).

With self-reflection and awareness, we can identify the root of the hesitancy that has our ego triggering the alarm system. Perhaps it is a core memory of a time you got knocked off balance—that time you bombed an audition for the school musical in fifth grade, or the disappointment of not getting into your dream college. We feel rejection keenly as youngsters, and many of us grew up in households where we heard "no" more than we did "yes." The word "no" becomes part of our own internal vocabulary, and our ego in particular uses it freely. We need to rewire those neural pathways, and learn how to say "yes, I can."

And what about the other side of the coin, that second inner voice, intuition? It is that gut feeling, which you know in your heart is never wrong, even if you try to ignore it and pretend you never heard it utter a word.

"Take the risk," it tells you. "Go for it. This is what you need to do. You know it to be true."

We don't always listen to our intuition. We more often operate from a place of ego. Peggy kept taking Sean back not because she was stupid—she heard her intuition; she knew it wasn't right—but she ignored that voice and let her ego take the lead.

Your intuition is a superpower, but it is underutilized because doing the right thing so often means doing the hard thing. We would prefer to not even try, because trying means we might fail. We are all human after all.

We become incredibly adept at ignoring our intuition. We distract ourselves when we hear it speak up; we come up with any number of ways to avoid those thoughts. But it is time to embrace that superpower. What a privilege it is to have access to that kind of infallible wisdom within ourselves. We must nurture it and access it, rather than pretend it's not there.

When you step into the gap, you will hear that beautiful inner voice loud and clear. Welcome it like an old friend. It is steady and strong and tells you what you know to be true, no matter how hard it is to hear. Your ego will at times trigger a conflict and try to get you to rationalize your way around your intuition. But in the gap, you can clearly distinguish between both voices—there is no fog or muddle. The answers reveal themselves, clear as day.

How many times have you heard a friend say, "I knew they weren't right for me," or "I knew I was making a mistake as I did it"? Stories of hindsight are examples where we push down our intuition and our ego wins out.

Your truth and your best path forward involve a combination of and a connection between your ego and your intuition. Let your intuition tell you what leaps are worth taking, and let your ego prepare you for a safe landing.

Do not ignore fear or worry, though let them inform you rather than rule you. Find that balance between your ego and intuition, the light and the dark, the yin and the yang. There is an old fable usually attributed to the Cherokee indigenous American people, in which a grandfather tells his young grandson that within us all exist two wolves battling away. The youngster asks which wolf wins, and the wise old man replies: "The one you feed."

Versions of the story often depict this internal conflict as a battle between good and evil, with a bloodthirsty wolf attacking a docile, peaceful wolf. I like to think of the wolves instead as ego and intuition, and the solution to this conflict is to feed them both. There is no courage without fear. You can be afraid and support your future self, and you can achieve equilibrium between your ego and your intuition.

Emotions should not control you. Your emotions are thoughts moving in motion. Some are slow and plodding, some are erratic and swift. When you sit in your stillness and enter the gap, your ego and intuition can guide you through these emotions, and you will learn to predict them and become comfortable with their movements.

You will also recognize that your emotions should not propel you into action. Emotions are there to be felt. It is your ego and intuition that inform your actions and what you put out into the world. Before you say the next thing, before you take the next action, before you ruminate and worry and obsess potentially over something that needs to change within your life, step into the gap. Close your eyes, listen to your inner voice, and reflect on your own beautiful nature.

Chapter Eight

MAKING THE GAP A HABIT

It's fascinating how a cat grooms itself. The way their eyes narrow when going into cleaning mode, as if in a ritual-induced trance. They are finely tuned grooming machines: their tongues are barbed and ideal for scraping dirt from their fur; they use their tiny incisors to nibble at debris between their toes; and they moisten their forepaws and use them like combs, wiping behind their ears and other parts they can't reach with their mouths.

I appreciate how diligent cats are at self-cleaning, spending close to half a day maintaining their coats, preventing parasites and infection, removing the smell of food, distributing oils evenly across their coats, and regulating their body temperature through the evaporation of saliva. Cats will also groom each other, forming and maintaining social bonds with their relatives and companions. The short- and long-term benefits of grooming are myriad for cats. But how did this habit form? Why is it so intrinsically ingrained in them?

Part of it is learned behavior—or nurture—with the various techniques for self-grooming passed down from mother to kitten. But the drive to engage in the habit so frequently is instinctual, tied into their nature. The process of natural selection instills a drive to maintain habits, which are beneficial for an animal's survival and ability to provide offspring.

Like cats, we are creatures of habit. We are adept at learning and mimicking the behaviors of our relatives and companions, and we have a strong inclination to repeat these behaviors when they provide short- and long-term benefits.

Our brains have even evolved habit-forming mechanisms. In a process known as "chunking," some neurons are responsible for noting the beginning and end of discrete elements of behavior, which are then grouped together into an automatic routine. This is why, after enough repetition and practice, a new habit will soon feel like second nature.

I want you to adopt the habit of stepping into the gap. I want it to become second nature to you, so you can reap its many benefits and lean on it for all the phenomenal support it can provide you. So, let's first try and understand the best way to form new habits, which is fortunately a well-studied area of psychology and brain science.

We all know that it can be tough to pick up a new habit, especially when it requires us to make time and expend effort. Going to the gym is a perfect example of this. Anyone who has managed to stick to a workout routine will tell you how many false starts, adjustments, and derailments they experienced before the habit finally stuck.

I believe there are a handful of components that complement the formation of habits, including proximal goal setting, situational cues, immediate rewards, flexibility, and getting support.

Proximal goal setting is a fancy term for establishing short-term, manageable goals. Studies that track learning in children frequently show that kids who set short-term (proximal) goals acquire skills more quickly and efficiently than those with long-term (distal) goals or no goals altogether.

Acquiring a new language is a great example of how proximal goal setting works. Consider three statements: the first, "I am going to learn Spanish," the second, "I am going to learn Spanish this year," and the third, "I am going to learn five new words in Spanish every day for a week."

Which of these statements would you say is better suited for forming the habit of learning a language? The first statement is ambitious, but you have not established any goals beyond the learning of Spanish. You have no timeline or plan, no commitment to motivate you. The likelihood of waking up and beginning your Spanish journey is relatively low. The second statement is an improvement—you have at least committed to a timeline, though you have left the door open for delays to your start date.

The third statement is fantastic for habit forming. You haven't even mentioned the ultimate, daunting goal of mastering an entire language. All you have done is set a perfectly achievable target that involves daily repetitions, which will trigger neural "chunking" and achievable goals that can be completed in the near-term, providing frequent gratification. These goals can then be modified as you improve your efficiency—perhaps your next sentence will be "I will learn how to conjugate three verbs in the first person present tense every day for a week" and so on.

As you grow in confidence and competency in the language—and begin to feel the buzz of acquiring a new skill—your goals can become loftier, your appetite for learning will increase, and your mastery of Spanish will snowball.

It's exactly the same for practicing awareness, stillness, and stepping into the gap. Instead of saying "I will spend more time stepping into the gap," it is preferable to say, "I will put aside ten minutes in the morning and the evening where I play in the gap, for a week."

Soon, you will grow to love stepping into the gap and experiencing all of its wonderful benefits. You will gain access to the gap with improving efficiency as your magical brain does its wonderful chunking, and stepping into the gap becomes one of your new habits that comes to you easily, like second nature.

The next step is the implementation of situational cues that trigger us to take part in a new habit. This phenomenon can occur naturally, without even thinking about it. Let's say you have a cup of coffee and a cookie each afternoon. The drinking of the coffee and the eating of the cookie are two different habits, but they become strongly linked together. When you switch on the kettle and prepare the coffee, you reach for the cookie jar without thinking. One habit leads seamlessly to another. You may even find that when you go to a friend's house in the afternoon and are offered a coffee, you feel like something is missing, and you have the strong urge for a sweet treat when the coffee arrives without a cookie on the side.

The same can go for stepping into the gap—if you attach it to a habit that is already well-formed, you are far more likely to adopt the gap into your daily routine. So, let's update our proximal goal sentence ("I will put aside ten minutes in the morning and the evening where I play in the gap, for a week").

Let's add some situational cues that we can attach to this new habit: "I will put aside ten minutes *directly after I brush my teeth* in the morning and the evening where I play in the gap, for a week."

Now, let's focus on immediate rewards, which is a great way to persist toward long-term goals. The long-term benefits of stepping into the gap are numerous—and we will get into them later in this chapter—though habit forming is really helped by first focusing on immediate rewards.

We know that working out regularly increases your overall health, longevity, and health span (i.e., the number of years lived with a high quality of life, free of degenerative conditions). We also know that long-term commitment to working out leads to a fit, attractive physique that may boost your confidence. However, these two factors are not the most powerful motivators when it comes to establishing a gym-going habit. Not many 25-year-olds worry about their bodies degrading in fifty years' time. And changes to your physique occur so gradually they are almost imperceptible on a week-to-week basis—there is no instant gratification to be found here.

So, instead of saying "I will go to the gym to prevent heart disease later in life," or "I will go to the gym to get a six-pack," you may be better off saying, "I will go to the gym because I love the endorphin-high and sense of achievement at the end of a workout."

When it comes to the gap, it's perfectly fine to say to yourself, "I will practice stepping into the gap because it will help me achieve balance in my personal and professional life." But when you are starting out and from the perspective of habit forming, it might be better to say to yourself, "I will practice stepping into the gap each day because it helps me reduce stress and activates the parasympathetic nervous system."

Flexibility is another important part of habit forming. Our lives are often hectic, and fitting in a new daily habit can be challenging. You are more likely to stick to a habit if you provide yourself some grace and wiggle room, instead of instilling a rigid plan that may be hard to stick with. A study that provided a cash incentive to gym-goers showed that people were less likely to stick to a routine if they received payment in a two-hour window than compared to those who were paid each day, regardless of timing.

So, when it comes to stepping into the gap, when you start out, it may be best to practice it at different times. For some people, a lunch break might be preferable to the early morning and vice versa. It's also okay to give yourself a couple of "pass cards" in a week—if you miss a session one day, then give yourself a pass, don't let it discourage you and derail your routine altogether.

Finally, I strongly encourage you to seek the support of others while you are on this journey. Perhaps you hire a mindfulness coach, or perhaps you simply tell your partner: "I am going to practice stillness each day. Please be aware of this need and help me maintain the environment I need to succeed."

You might even take it a step further and encourage your partner to let you know when they have noticed positive changes in your demeanor and attitude. This kind of reinforcement is great motivation. People who let others know they are planning on quitting smoking or drinking are more likely to stick with it, since now they have others holding them accountable. The same goes for adopting new positive habits in your life.

Hopefully, at this point, you have started playing in the gap, and you have noticed its benefits. You can see why it is worthwhile making the gap a habit. You love the feeling of becoming connected to your true and authentic self, and the ability to distinguish between your twin inner voices of ego and intuition.

Now it is time to practice. Be intentional about using the gap. Use the habit-forming tools we have just discussed to build sessions into your week; also lean on the gap when you encounter certain stressors. Has something triggered you? Has something set off your sympathetic nervous system, your flight or fight response? Is your heart rate elevated; are your palms sweaty; is your face flushed? Do you feel a lump forming in your throat or the desire to lash out?

First of all, you are human, and it is okay to feel this way. And second, these are all perfect opportunities to use your new superpower.

You now have the tools to recenter yourself and approach these stressful situations from a place of authenticity, with calm and clarity. You can access the comfort of the gap, submerging yourself in its warm, jewel-colored pools. The world is messy, and we are constantly overstimulated. But now you have this beautiful refuge from the madness, where you can check in with yourself and find balance.

You will keep going back to the gap once you experience its lightness. You will never forget what it is like to feel connected with your authentic self, and this bond grows increasingly firm and strong. Yes, you might have moments where you feel a little imbalanced or disconnected. But quickly—more quickly than you could have imagined—you learn how to connect back to yourself.

Lowering stress levels is one of the key short- and long-term benefits of the gap. We all know the immediate symptoms of stress. You feel jittery and anxious, you find it hard to focus, you are irritable, and you have a short fuse. The gap can help you readjust and reclaim peace in those moments.

From a long-term perspective, stress truly is a killer. Chronic stress is linked to all manner of behaviors that impact our health. Stress can encourage compulsive overeating and reliance on harmful substances like tobacco, drugs, and alcohol, which in turn raise the chances of developing serious diseases and conditions, including diabetes, heart disease, and cancer. Prolonged stress causes great mental anguish, opening the door to bouts of depression and anxiety.

Having a tool which wards off these many maladies through instantaneous stress reduction, well...that sounds too good to be true, doesn't it? But it's not. Making a habit of the gap does just that. Think about the act of going on vacation and how beneficial it can be to relax, unwind, disconnect, and recharge your batteries. Stepping into the gap is equivalent to taking several mini vacations a day, though the destination is within yourself. You have the ability to rejuvenate and replenish your soul, mind, and body. And it doesn't cost you a penny.

As you notice an improvement of your stress levels and mood, this will have a direct impact on your relationships. You will find yourself more patient, more compassionate, and more understanding. And you will have a renewed capacity to provide support to those around you without stretching yourself to a breaking point.

Your improved energy reserves will glow from within and emanate from the pores in your skin. And acting from a place of authenticity generates a magnetism that will draw people to you. You will feel a calm right to your core, right to the root of you. And there will be further, untold benefits that I cannot even name because they are unique to you.

For me, one of the most beautiful effects of finding the gap was a deep sense of gratitude. I felt gratitude that, with the support of the gap, the future felt less scary. In fact, it was the opposite; for the first time in a long time, I felt that magnificent, splendid thing: optimism.

So, let's start forming that habit. Take ten minutes to practice, whenever your schedule suits you. Studies show that it takes at least eighteen days to form a habit, so I invite you to commit that length of time to daily visits to the gap. If you need to pivot for a week, that's just fine. Sometimes breaks are helpful—you can often lift more weight than usual after a short hiatus from the gym—but the most important thing is to recommit and not let a break derail your progress altogether.

Ensure that you have created the right environment to play in the gap. If the dogs are barking, or the kids are just back from school, or the washing machine is about to ping, perhaps it's not the best time to enter the gap. Seek out those moments of peace, wherever you can find them.

Make this a priority. The world will not fall apart if you recuse yourself for a few stolen minutes. It is not selfish to take some "me time." In fact, it's the opposite—presenting your true self and acting from a place of mindfulness will improve the lives of those around you.

Set the stage for the process. Turn off the TV, switch off the music, eliminate any distractions. The rustle of trees, the hum of the ocean, the trickle of a stream, and other healing sounds of nature are just fine should total silence cause you disquiet. Perhaps sit on a bench outside, feeling the cool breeze on your skin. Remove headphones and ensure all of your sensory portals are open.

A key benefit of the gap is that it stops you from moving through life on autopilot. Sometimes the daily grind can become so dull and monotonous that we choose to ignore the act of living. I'm sure you've had those moments while reading a book when you have to go back a few paragraphs because you lost focus and ceased to absorb information. You can live your life this way too—you can flick on the autopilot setting and live without intention, you can cease to present your authentic self to the world. Stepping into the gap can shake you from this slumber and help you lead your life with purpose, through action rather than reaction.

Remember to give yourself some grace. This will not all happen overnight, and you will not get it right every time. The important thing is to understand whatever it was that threw you off balance. What was it that triggered you? How can you grow and learn and improve from this situation? When you make mistakes, allow yourself to learn from them, just before you practice self-forgiveness.

The one thing we can be certain of is that life is going to be a journey of ups and downs, peaks and valleys. One wave will crash after the next. But there is calm between them—and space for healing. Be patient and gracious. You are building an awareness muscle, and just like progress in the gym, it will take time to develop and see the results you desire. I bet that people will notice the change in you before you do, so listen to those around you. Accept their compliments when they come. Be open to kind words, and do not disregard or downplay them.

You are so much stronger than you ever give yourself credit for, and you are meant to go through this evolution. You're meant to grow, you're meant to expand, you're meant to change, just like the seasons. You can do this; you are fully capable.

Soon, this practice—this habit—will become a way of life. And it is something that no one can take away from you. It is embedded in who you are, as natural and innate as the blood flowing through your veins. You are truly connected to your truest self, and you are exactly where you need to be.

Chapter Nine

PROACTIVELY SUPPORTING YOUR FUTURE SELF

She begins in comfort, floating in the blissful cocoon of the womb. The fluid within the amniotic sac is warm, a consistent 98.6°F, and she has never known what it is to shiver. The biting cold has never numbed her fingers and toes. The uterine walls around her are soft and forgiving, cushioning her as her mother navigates the outside world. She knows no pain.

Her stomach is tethered to the placenta by a life-giving braid of blood vessels, transporting oxygen, water, sugars, proteins, fats, and myriad micronutrients, all she needs to nourish the multiplying cells in her young body. She has never felt the yearning pang of thirst, or the hollow ache of hunger.

The buffer of her mother's belly dissipates loud noises, absorbs the sun's harsh rays, and shields her from the patter of raindrops and the hands of strangers. She knows no discomfort. She knows no fear or anxiety.

Then one day everything changes. The warm fluid around her begins to dissipate, draining away from below. The walls of her home seem to move in on her, ever so slightly, before receding again. At first, she is not alarmed; the light squeezing feels like a gentle embrace.

Then the contractions become more intense and frequent, applying pressure to her head and body, forcing her downward toward the cervix. Her head is tilted forward until her chin touches her chest. The walls of her home continue to close in, squeezing her ever more tightly. Her head is thrust back now, the base of her skull touching the nape of her neck, and she is forced on through, beyond, out there, into the world.

All at once, her senses are overwhelmed. Bright light penetrates her eyelids, and the metallic taste of blood envelopes her tongue. A cacophony of sound barrages her ears: urgent voices, footsteps, the beeping of electronics, the clanking of medical equipment, punctuated by her own desperate cries. Cold air spills into her lungs and runs across her skin. Gloved hands grasp at her head and shoulders.

With a final spasm, her body is forced from the only home she has ever known in her short life, and the cold rushes across her body. She lets out wail after wail, overcome by the newness of it all. The unfamiliar intrudes every aspect of her being; the loss of comfort sends shockwaves through her; she is totally bamboozled by change.

This newborn could be me, or you, or all of us, since the trauma of birth is one we all share—a frightful bond that, along with death, is one of two inevitabilities experienced by the living.

We have already spoken about the influence trauma has on us all. We cannot totally protect ourselves from traumas; they happen to everyone. I believe that we are born suffering, and that we heal by creating positive experiences.

Perhaps it's helpful to view stepping into the gap as a form of confession. It is a sacred moment when you stop, you look within yourself, and you speak with total honesty and truth.

You locate those moments of trauma, and you note if they have exerted control over your actions. You identify the areas of your life where your ego has taken the reins and your intuition has been suppressed.

You cannot avoid trauma and suffering; they are a part of life, and the lessons in these pages will not change that. Traumas are a part of your journey and have an impact on your life. But you can have control over *how* they define you.

In 1987, then psychology PhD student Francine Shapiro was walking in the park and mulling over a distressing memory. She soon stopped to watch two squirrels playing in the trees. Her eyes followed the animals as they darted from branch to branch, their bodies twisting and turning like a pair of expert, bushy-tailed acrobats.

After just a few minutes of observing these creatures, Shapiro noted that she felt more relaxed and at peace. What caused this change in mindset? Was it the idyllic setting, the connection with nature? Perhaps, but she'd been walking through the lush and vibrant park for some time, and it was only when she stopped and visually engaged with the busy squirrels that the serenity set in.

Shapiro was suddenly struck by a deep insight, the kind that only comes along once or twice in a lifetime. She felt intuitively that the change in her mental state had something to do with the swift movement of her eyes, dancing from side to side to keep the squirrels in focus.

She knew that humans and other mammals move their eyes similarly in their sleep, a behavior known as "Rapid Eye Movement," or REM. She knew that some researchers had posited that REM played a role in memory processing.

Perhaps, Shapiro thought, therapists might exploit the relationship between eye movement and memory in order to help people with unresolved trauma. She worked with seventy volunteers and began to establish the procedures on which modern-day Eye Movement Desensitisation and Reprocessing therapy, or EMDR, is based.

I like to imagine that our brains process memories in a large room full of filing cabinets. Some memories are treasured or important, and the brain places these in the filing cabinets at the front of the room so we can access them easily and frequently. Other memories have less priority, and we must wander far down the aisles in order to retrieve them. Many things we experience are deemed superfluous to requirements and remain in cabinets for a few days or hours, before getting thrown out (this is why the majority of us do not have perfect recall). Meanwhile, other memories that we have not accessed for years soon expire. Research suggests that a lot of this organization might occur naturally during the REM phase of our sleep.

Traumatic memories break the rules of this well-ordered system. They jump from one filing cabinet to another, wreaking havoc. They might spend some time in a dusty old cabinet in the back of the room, and then they might spring forward, right into the nearest cabinet to the entrance, forcing you to relive the event as if it were happening then and there.

EMDR therapists attempt to harness the natural power of eye movement and other forms of bilateral stimulation, such as tapping. In a controlled therapy environment, an EMDR patient will be asked to recall the traumatic event while they follow a therapist's hand, which is waving from side to side in a particular pattern. In this way, the traumatic memory is encouraged to behave like any other memory; it is filed away in its appropriate cabinet where it stays put. The patient doesn't forget the trauma; they have simply reprocessed the memory. The bad thing happened, they cannot control it, but they are okay now, and they are going to be okay.

In the same way that EMDR can help us manage our memories and come to terms with the past, I believe that stepping into the gap can similarly help us process and prioritize our actions, as well as help us achieve the futures we desire. Our suffering and trauma provoke us to shut down and generate our responses on autopilot, reacting to the world instead of acting on our needs and desires with intention. Our fears and previous negative experiences encourage us to listen to our egos and disregard our intuition.

By stepping into the gap, checking in and connecting with our authentic truth, we can realign ourselves and act from a place of agency and intuition, helping us break the patterns of the past and cultivate a fulfilling future.

We all have baggage. We experience trauma and suffering the moment we are born. The ego will do its best to prevent further suffering, though it will frequently lose these battles. And the ego's effort to ward off trauma very often closes off the opportunity for pleasure, happiness, and fulfillment. We must acknowledge our trauma. There is no room for personal growth and transformation without suffering. But it cannot be the thing that guides or motivates us.

If you attempt to avoid suffering at all costs, you will also avoid happiness and fulfillment. Imagine if that baby at the beginning of the chapter never left the womb—she lived out the eighty or so years we get on average on this planet as a fetus. Sure, she would be safe and never know pain or discomfort. But she would never watch a sunset, she would never feel an embrace, she would never taste chocolate or go roller skating or receive a good grade or a promotion, she would never make new discoveries or start a family or run a marathon.

Challenges are what make us grow; they are what make us great. And when you have discovered yourself in the gap, you will be primed to take on challenges with a power and enthusiasm you have never experienced before. You will know how to function as the person you wish to be.

So, what does that future look like? Who is this future self? When you become fully aware, when your ego and intuition are working in a beautiful partnership, you can construct your future with intention; you are its skilled architect.

Dream big. Ask yourself: "Where is it that I see myself going? What do I want to call into my life? How do I want to show up in my life? What place do I want to show up from?" When you operate from your true, authentic self, the answers will vibrate through you loud and clear.

I want you to picture yourself five years from now waking up in the morning. I want you to describe the sheets you wake up in and what pajamas you are wearing. I want you to describe the feeling of the carpet or the floorboards beneath your feet as you make your way to the bathroom to brush your teeth and splash water on your face. Look in the mirror. Tell me who it is you see. What emotions can you read in those eyes? Tell me what clothes you put on as you dress. What colors, textures, and fabrics are you choosing to outwardly express your authentic self and your mood that day? How do the garments feel against your skin?

Walk me through to the kitchen. Is someone there to prepare breakfast with you? A partner or a spouse perhaps? Tell me about them. Are they a new person in your life, or have you been with them for a while? How do they make you feel? Is there chemistry between you— is it a wildfire or a gentle constant ember? Do they make you feel safe? Do they challenge you and encourage you in equal measure? Are you free to communicate openly and honestly? How do they champion you, and how do they receive your love? Do they express their gratitude and find ways to make you feel appreciated? And do they in turn feel supported by you?

Or perhaps you are alone and at peace? Will you grind coffee beans or brew tea for yourself, as you consider what lays ahead in the day? Are you reveling in a healthy solitude, grateful for the ability to focus on yourself?

Tell me what you have planned for the day. Tell me about the professional challenges that lie ahead. What tasks must you tackle, and how will you take them on? Are they intellectually stimulating? Are they creative or physically demanding? Does your role draw on long-held experience, or have you developed new skills in these past five years and taken on a fresh career?

And when the work is done, tell me where you go next. Tell me what hobbies or pursuits you are spending your free time on. Let me know how they enrich your body and your mind. Let me know if these activities excite you and fill you with confidence. Tell me if they bring you private and personal joy, or perhaps they are shared loves, and you are engaging in an active community of likeminded participants who expand your social life.

Tell me about your plans for the evening. Are you walking or driving to your next engagement? Where are you in the world? In a city, town, or rural area? Are you in a new state or country? Are you speaking in a new language as you interact with the locals?

Who are you meeting for drinks or dinner? Perhaps its family at home, or friends at a bar or restaurant. How do these people fit into your life? How do they complement you and support you? Tell me how they enrich the tapestry of your life. Tell me if they engage your mind, amuse you, and make you feel safe and loved. And tell me about the rewards you may feel for supporting them. How are you showing up for them and encouraging them to be the best versions of themselves?

And now, as you crawl into bed and prepare to rest for the night, tell me how many times you stepped into the gap that day. I would love for the answer to be at least ten times. Tell me where you did it—in the morning, on your lunch break, while you sat quietly in your yoga class, on a park bench in the sunshine. Tell me where you found stillness in the day, a place to pause and hone in on your thoughts until you found the spaces in between them to play and connect with your authentic self. Tell me about the process of distinguishing between your ego and intuition, and the peace and clarity you experienced when you identified the true motivations behind your actions, and the relief you felt when you realized that you were pursuing the right path. Tell how your time in the gap filled you with strength and an energy that vibrated through you, filling you with light that emanated from your very pores.

And now zoom out on that day and view it as a whole. What were the key emotional themes that flowed through the day? Was there kindness, passion, gratitude, and joy? Hone in on each of these and hold them in your mind. Tell me how good it feels to have these emotions feature so prominently in a 24-hour period. How life-changing must it be to have these beautiful feelings run through you and fuel your existence?

I want you to repeat this exercise whenever you feel uneasy and unsure about the path you are on. Explore the future and get to know the dominant themes—personal, professional, emotional—that keep appearing. These are your true aspirations and goals. They have not been chosen by others; they have been dreamt up by you alone, and they are what you must strive toward with an open mind and an open heart. If you wish, write this all down in a journal. The practice of what I call "future drafting" is a great way to analyze and identify your true priorities. You can look back on how details may have changed over time and note which aspirations and emotions remain constant.

People can and do change, and it is helpful to be receptive to this. The cells in our skin and blood are replaced in a matter of days and weeks, and the cells in our bones, fat, and muscles regenerate every decade or so. Our brains continue to rewire themselves as we age and as our environments present us with new challenges, constraints, opportunities, and information.

In his book, *The Brain That Changes Itself*, neurologist Norman Doidge explains the incredible ability of the brain to overcome disability through a process called neuroplasticity. Doidge provides several case studies of patients recovering from brain injuries (including strokes) that have damaged or killed parts of the brain. Over time, patients showed the ability to regain speech or mobility in affected limbs, as control of these behaviors was taken over by new areas of the brain. Doidge goes on to reflect on how neuroplasticity may be triggered by subtle changes to our environment, including new cultures or forms of education.

The outdated traditional model of the brain held that you receive your full complement of neurons as an infant, and by young adulthood, your neural pathways are pretty much set in stone. What comes after this, the old model claimed, is the slow decline or neural degeneration. But new studies show that the brain might never stop making neurons, and the breakthroughs in the science of neuroplasticity frequently illustrate how adept our brains are at adapting to new challenges.

Embrace the changes in your tastes, goals, and ambitions. The world will change, and so will you; it is part of our physiology. But remind yourself of the things that remain consistent in your drafts of the future, as these are your core values and beliefs.

Now you have a picture of your future self in mind; use this as your North Star, your own personal lighthouse that navigates you across the ocean of your life, when it is placid and welcoming, or violent and stormy.

Let it be your guide. And when you contemplate tough decisions, ask: How would this path support my future self? How am I working toward that vision of the future? When I sit in stillness and step into the gap, is my authentic self telling me that I am operating from a place that will support this vision of the future?

As we've discussed, change will come in abundance; you will adapt, evolve, and even your brain will rewire. So, repeat this future drafting and practice it week to week, month to month, year to year. Ensure you are constantly checking in with yourself and you are keeping that beautiful picture of the future in clear view, in sharp relief. When you do this, you will slowly start to notice subtle changes in yourself. Over time, you will begin to become the person in that future draft—you will start to adopt her habits and assemble the skills necessary to conduct her daily life.

And don't worry, you will falter. The suffering, the struggles, the trauma of existence will throw you off course. Strong winds will pull you away from that lighthouse, and at times, it will appear as a pinprick on the horizon. But it will always be there, and now you have this superpower to rely on. Keep going back to the gap to recenter yourself and ensure that you are operating from your authentic truth.

Keep dreaming, and dream big dreams. I promise you, the dreams that you have now are not nearly big enough. When people ask me what my dreams are for the future, I tell them: "I am not able to really articulate that; my words have not caught up with my imagination. But these are the things that I'm working on right now to continue to grow and be of service and to support myself, the people around me, and my community."

I know I am going to make mistakes, and you are too. They are going to be tough to swallow and may be painful at times. But let these missteps allow us to grow. Stagnation, consistency, and complacency are where dreams go to die.

So continue to visualize, continue to dream, and continue to get uncomfortable. Challenge yourself in the gentlest as well as the largest of ways. Let "I don't know if I can do that, but I'm going to try" become your mantra. Some of the most enormous tasks ahead of us appear trivial when we overcome them; they recede in the rearview mirror.

You are not too late. You are not too old. You have not done the things that you have done for no reason at all. This has all been part of the journey. You are beautiful just as you are, and you are just as you're meant to be. And that future self is waiting for you. Enjoy the journey. Enjoy it from this moment forward. You will begin to manifest the wondrous change you have imagined.

Chapter Ten

CORE RELATIONSHIPS THROUGH THE GAP

In November 2012, more than 200 people played a global game of Telephone to mark International Games Week. There is a good chance you played the game as a kid, and you probably remember how it works: a group assembles in a line or a circle, and one player whispers a message into another's ear. That player passes on what they hear to the next, and so on down the line until the final player says the message out loud.

That year, participants called in from twenty-four libraries in more than a dozen countries across multiple continents, and the whole thing took place over twenty-six hours. Players at the St Kilda Library in Melbourne, Australia, kicked off the game with the Plato quote, "Life must be lived as play." The message passed through a handful of other Australian libraries, and became increasingly garbled, changing to "Love like a play," "Eat while we live," and "Big purple dove."

Subsequent players in China passed the message "Very good to have a walk" onto players in India, whose phrase "Don't worry, be happy" made it to Uganda, then Belarus. The phrase was imperfectly passed on by participants in Romania, Serbia, Bosnia and Herzegovina, South Africa, the United Kingdom, Italy, Canada, and Colombia, before players at Homer Public Library in Arkansas, United States, delivered the final message: "He bites snails."

While Telephone is just a fun game, it shows us something important about the transmission of information and how difficult it is to get it right. Something as simple as copying a short sentence can easily go awry, and we see similar errors crop up all the time in both nature and culture.

Our cells mess up DNA replication when copying genes. These mutations can be catastrophic, leading to the demise of an organism, or beneficial, providing an advantage that is then passed on through generations via the process of natural selection. In the 1980s, evolutionary biologist Richard Dawkins coined the term "meme" to describe units of cultural transmission such as beliefs and behaviors that are altered by biases and other selective cultural pressures. Dawkins's idea became a kind of self-fulfilling prophecy, since the word "meme" itself has adopted a new meaning and is most commonly used today in reference to images, GIFs, and short videos that are shared widely on the internet.

There are any number of pressures that influence and alter the meaning of an idea or message when communicated between individuals. The game of Telephone shows us that people are often surprisingly inefficient and get simple ideas from A to B.

Sometimes, the breakdown in communication is not caused by a user error like mishearing or misspeaking, but by our own subconscious biases. Phrases like "You're hearing what you want to hear" and terms like "selective hearing" describe our ability to bend or manipulate the words of others to conform to our own wishes. Meanwhile, our tone of voice and body language might often be saying one thing while our words say another. Research suggests that around half of the signals we send and receive in a conversation are made up of non-verbal cues.

The picture is further muddied when you consider that two people might have differing expectations for the purpose of a conversation. In his book

Supercommunicators: How to Unlock the Secret Language of Connection, Pulitzer-prize winning journalist Charles Duhigg argues that there are three distinct categories of conversation, namely: practical, emotional, and social.

In practical conversations, we exchange information, make plans, and discuss solutions to problems. Two parents figuring out how they are going to pick up one kid from school and another kid from soccer practice while the car is in the shop would qualify as a practical conversation. An emotional conversation is more about expressing feelings and being understood. In this scenario, one individual might be looking to another for empathy rather than fixes to their problems. Social conversations generally involve swapping experiences and ideas with one another—from congenial chats about a recent holiday, to hot button topics like religion and politics.

Duhigg says that a lot of miscommunication arises because, often unbeknownst to them, two individuals are engaged in different types of conversation.

For example, you might let your partner know how disappointed you are after a bad job interview.

"You'll be fine," your partner might respond. "There will be more interviews to come. Ask them for any feedback that might improve your chances in the next one."

Your partner is of course right, but this doesn't change the fact that you are disappointed and crestfallen. You had started to fantasize about getting this particular job already, and it feels like a real punch in the gut that this version of your future has been closed off.

Why do your partner's words not quite help in this situation? Perhaps it's because they are engaged in a practical conversation, while you are attempting an emotional one. You may be more receptive to advice on how to improve your job-finding skills down the line, but at this moment, you need a different kind of support. You need your partner to know how much you wanted it and how much this sucks.

I'm sure you will be able to think of other such times when the individuals were simply not converging on a conversation type. Many a Thanksgiving dinner has been ruined by discussions about political elections or a family member's lifestyle choices, which blurred the lines between emotional and social conversation.

So many of the problems we encounter in our personal, private, and professional lives stem from bad communication.

And I would suggest that, oftentimes, miscommunication will occur not just because two individuals might be having different types of conversation, but because you yourself might not be sure what type of conversation you are having.

We need to stop and ask ourselves: What do we want from this dialogue? Do I want emotional support? Practical advice? To ensure that my ideas are being understood? If you can get clear on your own needs in a communication scenario, you massively increase the chances that the person you are speaking with will get closer to understanding your point of view.

And this is where stillness, awareness, and stepping into the gap come in. Before I throw myself headfirst into a discourse, I often stop and give myself a moment. In the gap, I can access my true, authentic self and discover what I really want to say. I can check to see if I need to transfer the reins from my ego to my intuition. I can ensure that I am not reacting; rather I am acting with intention. I can take a moment in time to select the right words.

Because words *really* matter. We must be careful with them. They are a powerful tool with which you outwardly express your inner self. If you are clumsy or thoughtless with words, not only do you stand the chance of hurting someone, you also risk conveying a wholly inaccurate image of yourself to the world.

I'm not saying this is easy. You are going to mess up and make mistakes. But the gap provides you a beautiful ability to recognise those errors right away, allowing you the chance to rectify them instead of having them compound the issue.

On a daily basis, I will stop, step into the gap and ask myself, "Is that truly what I wanted to communicate?" And sometimes the answer is *no*, which is totally fine.

"Okay," I say to myself. "I want to do this a little differently. Let me try this again."

And this is why I call the gap a superpower. Imagine how much time you will save and how much unnecessary confusion you will avoid if you don't let miscommunications snowball and go unresolved! Awareness of the gap is a true gift, providing you the ability to try again; whereas in the past you may have soldiered on, unaware that you were reacting and not acting from a place of intention and authenticity.

From this new vantage point, you will no longer have to constantly fight fires, as one mistake leads to several others in an exponential manner. Living in "react mode" leads to fear and anxiety, and it is a difficult pattern to break.

"What's going to hit me next?" you might think. "I've seen this before. One bad thing leads to the next, and it's going to ruin my day. I got a ticket this morning on my way to work, and now the whole day is going to just erupt and turn bad. I'm late for my first meeting, so now I'll be late for all of my other meetings."

Giving yourself the opportunity to reset and recalibrate means you will no longer catastrophize and will be clear-minded in the way you communicate with others, rather than giving off stress and anger, which will ultimately mean you are misunderstood.

So instead of having life live us, we're going to live life. We are going to take life by the reins. We are going to proactively remind ourselves now that we have this powerful awareness. We can calmly determine what we need to do next.

Not getting your point across—not feeling seen or heard—leads to pent up anger and frustration. Think about how babies communicate their needs before they find their words. They cry, right? No matter what it is—if they need protection from the cold, if they are thirsty or hungry, if they need their diaper changed, if they are gassy, if they feel afraid or alone and need company and caresses—whatever it may be, their ability to get their point across is so limited that they have no choice but to fall back on that most primal form of communication: crying out. With such a blanket response to a multitude of needs, parents often have to go through a bit of trial and error to figure out what's wrong.

But you know what? The same goes for us as adults. If we don't stop to find out what our true needs are, if we don't attempt to act from an authentic place and choose the right words, we can become like children— resorting to frustration and yelling, while others around us scramble to figure out exactly what's bothering us.

And when the dust settles, we are left asking for forgiveness. We are constantly apologizing. Let's think about apologies for a minute. When you receive an apology, it might feel good, because it is a recognition that someone else is wrong. Similarly, if you give someone an apology, and you receive forgiveness, you might feel a sense of relief; you might feel a little less guilty. You hurt someone, you apologized and were forgiven, and the issue is now in the past.

Where in any of this is personal growth? How has receiving an apology made you a better, more functional person? And how has giving an apology made you any less likely to mess up again in the future?

Don't get me wrong, I do believe that apologies have their place. But I also argue that they are limited, and we tend to put far too much emphasis on them. We rely on them as a quick fix, a cure-all. We end up telling ourselves, "If I mess up, I need to apologize in order to move on," instead of getting to the root of the issue and ensuring that we don't repeat past mistakes or negative patterns of behavior.

I want you to apologize to yourself less. I want you to remove the word *sorry* from your inner vocabulary. I want you to stop regretting your past actions and instead ask how you might prevent those actions from occurring again. Instead of saying, "I can't believe I did that; I'm so stupid," ask, "Where was I operating from in order for this reaction to have surfaced?" In this way, you will no longer sit paralyzed in an unhelpful cycle of self-flagellation and self-forgiveness. You will now move forward from a place where past errors inform future success.

Operating from a place of intention is among the most liberating changes you can make. Give yourself the space and the grace before you speak to ensure that you are communicating your authentic truth. Ask yourself, do I wish to engage in a practical discussion or an emotional one? And tell this to the person you are talking to, so they are on the same page and aware of your expectations. Say what is on your mind, giving yourself a second in order to choose your words carefully.

Sometimes, the words won't come, or you might be unsure of them. You can often tell if someone is saying something they don't mean, or when they are blurting out a half-baked opinion they are forming in real time.

I find it better to say nothing at all in these instances. If I can't find the words, I will say to my partner: "I need to think this through. I'm having a feeling. I'm experiencing something, and I don't have the words just yet to communicate what it is. I want to look at it a little bit more. I want to understand it better before I simply blurt it out and verbally vomit all over the place. I don't want to do that anymore because it doesn't feel good when somebody does that to me."

We, as human beings, are responsible for our feelings and emotions. And that is a heavy responsibility to bear sometimes. But trust me, the burden becomes so much lighter when you understand what those emotions, thoughts, and feelings mean to you—and where they are coming from. You now have this tool to help you understand them and dig a little deeper into them.

It took me years to discover the level of responsibility I have over my emotional state of being. For so long, I thought that others dictated how I felt through their treatment of me. I was a blank page, and others were writing my story for me, and I had little control over what they wrote, be it kind and constructive words, or cruel and hurtful ones.

I was living my life as children do, totally reliant on their parents to set the tone for their emotional wellbeing: "I'm sad, make me happy! I'm bored, entertain me! This is broken, fix it for me!" When I lost my father at a young age, I soon learned how powerful a role he played in creating a rich and colorful emotional landscape for me, which I had taken for granted. Grief truly is love with nowhere to go.

For the longest time, I did not know what to do with my emotions. I just knew how to feel them. I didn't know where they came from, how to channel them, or how to process them. Now that I have access to the gap, I can do all these things and more. I can identify why I feel certain emotions, take responsibility for them, and respond to them with intention. I now choose my words carefully and ensure that I express my authentic self. I speak no more or no less than I did in the past. But I listen a whole lot more, and I communicate with meaning. My words are so much more beautiful, impactful, and powerful because they have intention behind them.

And I tell you what, this practice rubs off on people. Others can tell right away if you are showing up as your authentic self. You are far more engaging and magnetic when you speak with truth. People want to learn this skill from you, and they will feel drawn to you.

When you speak with truth and intent, people may not like what you say, but at least you will be understood. And man does that feel good.

It has fundamentally changed my relationships, and I can see those around me adopting the same posture. Sometimes, if I feel overwhelmed and I know I am not going to communicate the best version of myself to my children, I say to them: "I'm feeling a big feeling now, and I don't know how to talk about it in the best way. Mama's gonna take a timeout and come back in a second. I need to do this so I don't do or say anything I might have to apologize for."

Your relationship with your children deepens and reaches a higher level of understanding when they see you as human, rather than as an infallible, omniscient caretaker.

I take myself away, have a sit down, or splash some water on my face. I reset and recenter. I connect with that awareness, and I unpick the root of my feelings. I find the right words, and I share them when I am ready.

My kids have seen how helpful these timeouts are for me, and they have started using them.

Something will work them up. They know they have a lot of feelings running through them, even if they don't have the words for each emotion yet.

I'll ask them if they want to talk about it, and they sometimes say: "Not yet, Mom. I need a timeout." And I'll reply: "Good for you, honey. I will be here to hold space when you're ready."

This brings me so much joy. I feel that I have given them such a powerful gift that will provide huge value for the rest of their lives.

I do the same thing with my partner. If I'm having difficulty communicating, I prefer to pause rather than muddle on through. I might say: "Look, when we get really worked up, sometimes I'm going to need you to allow me that space." He has started to take space now, too, and finds it so helpful.

It's in this space that we can identify instances where we are having different kinds of conversations than each other. And you might see that you are placing expectations on the conversation—or on your partner—that they are totally unaware of, so no wonder the dialogue has become so confusing and frustrating. You can now come back to the conversation and ensure that your goals and expectations are aligned from the beginning.

The same goes for conversations in the workplace. My relationships with my colleagues improved immensely when I started honing my communication skills through awareness, intention, and frequent visits to the gap. Workplaces can be areas of high energy, tension, and anxiety. Such environments call for stillness, calm, and creativity, all of which are provided in abundance by the gap.

I find creativity and productivity come more easily from a state of calm and stillness than a place of overstimulation. Being busy or talkative does not necessarily mean you are being productive—practitioners of active procrastination will tell you as much. Stillness has and forever will be the most productive place you can be. It's where creativity comes to flourish.

So, before you assign or delegate those additional tasks, check in with your employees. The next time you have a meeting, pause before you walk in the room or jump on the zoom, and check your energy. Are you bringing in a flustered vibe that will unsettle the whole team? Or are you bringing calm and confidence that you can share with others?

Sometimes when I start a meeting—in the conference room or on a video call—I will open with a pause and a deep breath. I know, it sounds crazy, but try it. Allow people to hear you draw that breath, hold it, and let it go. First off, this will be quite disarming. They will stop looking surreptitiously checking their phones, or worrying about the multitude of tasks that this meeting is keeping them from. You will have their full and undivided attention.

"Are you okay?" they might ask.

"Sure, I'm just taking a moment to bring calm into this day," I've replied before. "I'm taking a moment to breathe. Please feel free to join me."

And often people thank me, telling me they didn't realize until they stopped to calm themselves that they were carrying so much tension.

So, communicate your new practices to your friends, family, and colleagues. Let people know that you are operating with intention, authenticity, and awareness. Invite them to join you. Be their leader, be their inspiration. Be grateful for all that stepping into the gap has given you, and pay it forward. It is the most magical gift you can give.

Chapter Eleven

THE PATH TO LEADERSHIP AND POWER THROUGH THE GAP

Fledgling programmer Dave Thomas was studying computer science at Imperial College London in the late 1970s. It was an exciting time for computing; major leaps in microprocessing allowed for the rollout of the first PCs, bringing computers into the homes of the masses for the first time.

Thomas was eager to lap up knowledge wherever he could find it, and each week he looked forward in particular to working under research assistant Greg Pugh, who was among the most talented developers at the university.

Something curious was playing on Thomas's mind. He'd noticed that wherever Pugh went, he carried around a rubber duck with him. When Pugh arrived at work, he'd take the duck from his bag and place it next to his keyboard, with the toy's eyes trained on the computer screen. Thomas had noticed the ritual day after day, until enough was enough—he had to ask about it.

"Hey Greg," Thomas said. "What's with the rubber duck?"

"I was wondering when you were going to ask about that," Pugh said. "It helps me learn."

Pugh went on to explain that if ever he encountered a bug in his programming that he couldn't immediately see a fix for, he would stop and explain each line of code to the duck. He would assume, rightly, that the duck had no prior knowledge of computer science, and he would therefore articulate his coding in clear and easy-to-understand terms. He would teach the duck about programming. Pugh explained that the process of teaching the duck and talking through his problems would help him uncover solutions that hadn't jumped out at him previously.

Thomas was suitably impressed and began to adopt the method, which greatly helped his programming. He would go on to write *The Pragmatic Programmer: From Journeyman to Master*, a highly regarded guide to software development that is used as a textbook in computer science courses at universities around the world. Thomas wrote about Pugh in this book, and "rubber ducking" is now a commonly used term among developers who practice learning-by-teaching, which is also called the "protégé effect" or "plastic platypus learning" (the particular toy used is obviously not important!).

People have relied on the power of this method of learning for thousands of years. Ancient Roman philosopher Seneca the Younger came up with the proverb "*Docendo discimus*" or "by teaching we learn."

American theoretical physicist Richard Feynam once said: "If you cannot explain something in simple terms, you don't understand it." This quote forms the basis of the Feynman Technique, a form of learning in which you attempt to explain your working in terms a child could grasp.

Learning by teaching forces us to actively retrieve what we have been taught—including those lessons that may have begun to fade in our memories. We are then required to package, contextualize, and articulate these lessons clearly, in simple language, that bolsters both the student's understanding of the topic as well as our own.

Why do I tell you all of this? I want you to find your "rubber ducks" and teach them about the gap. I want you to share your new ability to find stillness, authenticity, and heightened awareness with your friends, family members, and colleagues. In doing so, you will hone your own abilities, you will improve the lives of those around you, and you will naturally emerge as a leader in your own community.

I want you to teach those you care for about the 6,000 thoughts we have each day, and about the gap that exists between each thought. Show them that this gap acts as a moment of reprieve from overstimulation, chaos, and stress. Tell them to think about the gap as the space between two words in a sentence, or the calm waters between two waves building in the ocean. Tell them that accessing this arena will allow them to approach the problems in their lives with radical agency. Explain that the world is brimming with distractions, diversions, and the nagging pull of empty dopamine hits. Let them know that, if they are looking for change, you can help them.

Teach them about the importance of identity and the power of self-recognition. Let them know how our identity needs to be nurtured and examined—it must not be taken for granted or neglected; otherwise we may stray from it and end up in crisis. Encourage them to sit still and ask the questions: "Do you feel comfortable? Do you feel comfortable in your own skin? Do you feel comfortable in my job, with your partner, in those clothes, in that city?" Let them know that the answers to those questions will lead them to a better understanding of their core values and beliefs.

Encourage them to describe themselves less in relation to others (I am a mother, a daughter, a lawyer, a friend) and with more personal vocabulary (I am kind, I am loyal, I am nurturing, I am funny) in order to strengthen their sense of identity.

Tell them about the struggles that women live through today, and how the twin pressures of conforming to "traditional timelines" and professional goals can lead to unrealistic and imposed expectations for womanhood. Tell them how a predetermined set of feminine characteristics handed down by society makes it tough for women to lead authentic lives. Tell them how the gap can help them regain radical agency and start living the lives they truly want, rather than the lives they are told they should lead. Tell them that their uniqueness should be celebrated instead of cowed.

Teach them how to become aware of the gap. Tell them about the forgotten sixth sense, proprioception, and the benefits of nurturing and connecting with this sense, as we regularly do for the senses of touch, taste, hearing, sight, and smell. Teach them that becoming acutely aware of our limbs in space will help us engage with the present moment, where we can more easily access the gap.

Teach them to pick a comfy spot ten times a day where they can momentarily unplug from devices and distractions. Tell them to imagine floating in water, released from the pull of gravity, finding a beautiful buoyancy and an enveloping sensation that keenly connects them to the present moment—as a cold plunge does. Teach them how to breathe and reset their bodies under the control of the parasympathetic nervous system. Reassure them that emptying the mind is not the goal here, rather we are focusing on letting thoughts pass and noticing the gap in between them.

Reassure them that accessing the gap not only helps with big problems or emotional traumas—it is there to support you whenever you need, including trivial bumps in the road. Tell them that it is okay to fail, because failure is a key ingredient to success, and overcoming defeat gives us confidence.

Remind them that humans have an innate and ancient requirement to rest and reset on a daily basis, as evidenced by historical sleep patterns and in the needs of children. Let them know that the structure and hectic schedules of modern life rarely allow for these moments of repose, and it is up to us to make space for them through intentional mindfulness. Tell them that these pauses can last as long as a meditation session or as short as a brief beat before we speak.

Teach them about the complementary roles our ego and intuition play in our decision-making. Let them know that these twin voices deserve equal attention, and it is within the gap that you can distinguish between their messages. Tell them that the ego has their best interests at heart but will always come from a place of risk aversion, often advising you to maintain the status quo and suppressing personal growth. Let them know that your intuition is never wrong and can help guide you toward the right path, even if that means taking a leap into the unknown.

Encourage them to make the gap a habit, by setting short-term achievable goals, adopting situational cues for practicing mindfulness, and focusing on the benefits of the gap, including problem-solving, finding peace, and calling in health benefits through stress reduction. Let them know that entering the gap will become easier with time and practice. Teach them how stepping into the gap frequently will jolt them out of autopilot, allowing them to live their lives with intention, rather than having their lives live them.

Explain how the gap will allow them to proactively support their future selves. Teach them the benefits of "future drafting" and imagining in keen detail a vision of their future that pleases them and brings them joy. Encourage them to practice future drafting frequently, and reassure them that visions of the future will change as they do. Tell them to pay close attention to the aspects of these visions that remain unchanged, as here they will find their core values and beliefs. Tell them that this vision of the future will act as their lighthouse, guiding them through foggy, choppy seas. Remind them to dream big, and that there is no limit to what we should wish for ourselves.

Talk to them about how the gap improves our communication with others, and how this can transform our lives and our relationships. Teach them about the importance of identifying the kinds of conversations we wish to have, whether practical, social, or emotional, and how we should aim for all parties to have similar expectations from a dialogue. Let them know how transformative choosing your words with intention can be, and how sometimes, it is better to not speak at all.

Tell them to take timeout or a pause before they talk in order to collect their thoughts and communicate with clarity. Encourage them to apologize less and view their mistakes as opportunities for growth.

Finally, teach them all the wonderful lessons the gap has taught you that are not contained in the pages of this book. We are all unique beings with our own skills and learnings to offer. I have shared what the gap has meant for me, but I can only begin to imagine what it might offer you. And I cannot wait to find out. So share your personal experiences with me, your loved ones, your colleagues, and whoever else will listen. Spread your truth far and wide.

You are now proactively supporting your future self, almost subconsciously. The ripples of peace are emanating from your core and touching every aspect of you, to the furthest reaches of your being. Hopefully, your new ability to connect with your authentic self fills you with the confidence to take control of your life and live it with intention.

I suspect that people will see a change in you. "What have you done?" they might ask you. "What's changed? What have you started to call into your life? What magic supplement are you taking?"

You can tell them that it's no mystical lotion or potion.

"I've just utilized this beautiful practice that was a part of who I was already," you can say. "I've tapped into this profound wisdom inside of me that was there all along; I just needed to make my way back to it."

Whereas the constant stream of thoughts and stimulations in your life made your mind muddy, access to the gap has purified the waters; they are now crystal-clear. You feel comfortable in yourself and have renewed confidence.

You are connected, in tune, and balanced. So, what are you going to do with this superpower? What decisions are you going to make operating from this place of confidence? The possibilities are endless. The big, lingering questions become less daunting, and you can address them with poise and power. You now know you can stop, find your stillness, take a deep breath, and say: "I'm going to step into this gap and figure out what the next right action is."

As you teach what you have learned to those around you, and as you emanate this newfound sense of identity, you will find that you become a natural leader. People are attracted to authenticity, and those that act and speak with intention, honesty, and wisdom. You will become positively magnetic; people will feel drawn toward you and relish your company.

You will inspire them. Think carefully about how you will step up to this new responsibility. And consider what new roles and directions you may take in response. In my case, I was inspired to return to yoga after a long hiatus from semi-consistent practice.

As I grew in confidence through the gap—and the idea of leadership began to sit right with me—the yoga studio called me back. I completed my training and became able to share this gift with others. What gifts and skills will you share?

Sharing our gifts is transformative, enabling you to elevate and empower those around you, filling you with great pride and gratitude. And by teaching your "rubber ducks," you will in turn grow more confident and adept in your own talents.

With the gap, you have unlocked a superpower that allows you to connect with your truest self. You have the potential to become a magnetic leader who shares their unique gifts with the world. You are able to cultivate a beautiful balance in your life—you have found the power and productivity of stillness and departed from the rat race we are encouraged to run from a young age.

You can take a different, more fulfilling and deliberate path.

You know that trauma and suffering is a part of life, and now you will rise as a leader and take on challenges with confidence, bravery, and a new sense of capability.

"Yes, I'm going to endure hardships," you may say. "Work isn't always fun; it's not always easy, but I'm doing this with intention. And I'm not going to race through life, I'm going to enjoy life, I'm going to be present, and I'm going to truly understand what it is that I'm working so hard towards."

The challenges will be varied: from the gift of nurturing children, to the joy of creating art, to the accomplishment of starting a new business. The gap can help us with every kind of challenge there is. Whatever you create is your legacy; it's your name; it is what you leave behind in this world. The decisions we make in life add to this legacy, and acting with intention ensures that those decisions are the right ones for us. The gap can help us guarantee that what we put out in the world is a true reflection of our authentic selves, as well as our core beliefs and values. I am so eager to learn what you put into the world. We all want to hear it in your words. We want to hear it in your thoughts. Your own experience is unique and will never be lived again.

And remember: The goals you set are the finished product, but it's your intentions that will carry you along this way. Ask yourself constantly, "What is my intention behind this action?" And enjoy the comfort and confidence of taking this journey with deliberate steps.

I hope you enjoyed this part of the journey, which we took together. I hope you've enjoyed the practice of stepping into the gap. I hope you have enjoyed understanding how incredibly strong you are. I hope that you are smiling as you read, because you have never felt more connected to your true self. Remember that there is nobody else like you on this planet. You are a unique, beautiful creation, and I cannot wait to see all that you choose to share. I cannot wait to hear your stories and learn of the relationships you have cultivated and nurtured.

You are now vibrating on a higher frequency, and the universe is sending you abundance. The waters of your mind are crystal-clear, and you can see your beautiful reflection in magnificent detail. You have 6,000 opportunities a day to feel this way, so step into the gap and enjoy.

ABOUT AUTHOR

Tessa Arnold leads individuals to Step into the Gap, transforming and reclaiming their lives. After a transformative shift triggered by multiple losses in her own life, Tessa left her 12-year global banking career to study the mind-body connection, eventually co-founding SnapBack Energy and Balance of You Co. As a certified Ayurvedic Health Coach, her work is deeply informed by her expertise in neuroplasticity and holistic wellness.

Tessa's mission is to empower listeners, sparking transformative conversations that shift their perspectives and allow them to navigate life's challenges. Through her unique blend of entrepreneurship and holistic living, Tessa embodies self-discovery and impactful change in the people she serves.

www.ingramcontent.com/pod-product-compliance
Lightning Source LLC
Chambersburg PA
CBHW020855090426
42736CB00008B/381